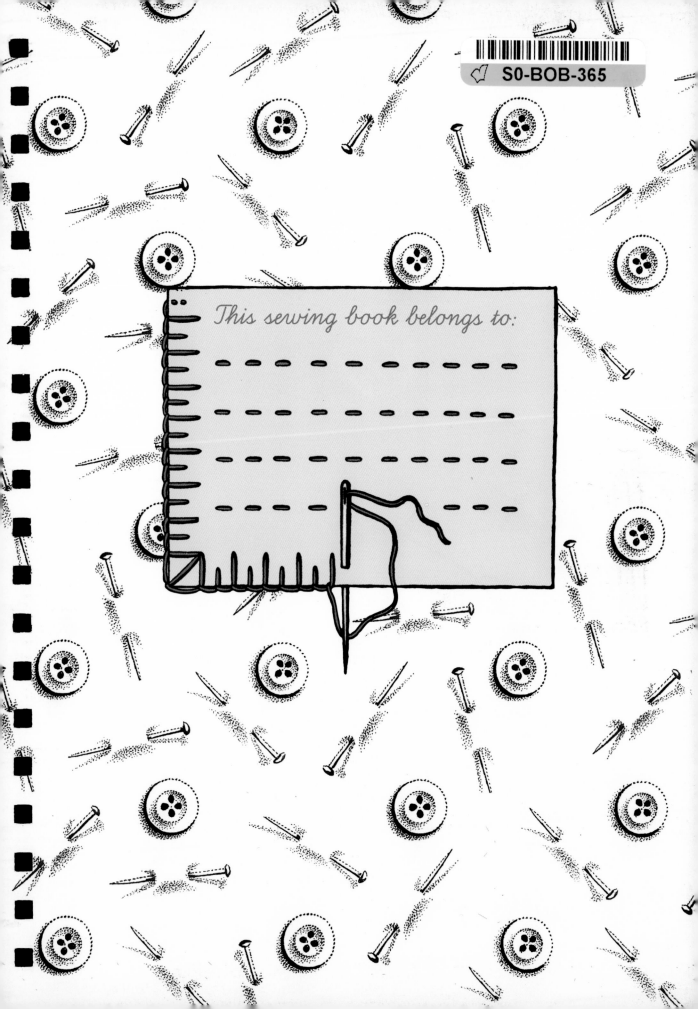

This sewing book belongs to:

STC CRAFT | A MELANIE FALICK BOOK

STEWART, TABORI & CHANG

NEW YORK

SEE
and
SEW

A SEWING BOOK FOR CHILDREN

TINA DAVIS

EDITOR: DERVLA KELLY
DESIGNER: TINA DAVIS
PRODUCTION MANAGER: KIM TYNER AND DEVON ZAHN

LIBRARY OF CONGRESS CATALOGING-IN-PUBLICATION DATA:

DAVIS, TINA.
SEE AND SEW : A SEWING BOOK FOR CHILDREN / TINA DAVIS.
P. CM.
ISBN I-58479-491-7
I. SEWING--JUVENILE LITERATURE. I. TITLE.

TT712.D38 2006
646.2--DC22

2005020834

COMPILATION COPYRIGHT © 2006 BY TINA DAVIS

PUBLISHED IN 2006 BY STEWART, TABORI & CHANG
AN IMPRINT OF HARRY N. ABRAMS, INC.

CREDIT FOR COPYRIGHT HOLDERS LISTED ON PAGES 146-147

THE TEXT OF THIS BOOK WAS COMPOSED IN SCALA AND SCALA SANS

PRINTED AND BOUND IN THAILAND
10 9 8 7 6 5 4 3 2

HNA
harry n. abrams, inc.
a subsidiary of La Martinière Groupe

115 WEST 18TH STREET
NEW YORK, NY 10011
WWW.HNABOOKS.COM

EVERY EFFORT HAS BEEN MADE TO OBTAIN
PERMISSION FROM PUBLISHERS AND COPYRIGHT
HOLDERS OF PREVIOUSLY USED MATERIALS.
CREDIT IS GIVEN WHEN KNOWN ON PAGES 146–147.

ALL THE PROJECTS IN THIS BOOK
SHOULD BE MADE WITH THE ASSISTANCE AND
SUPERVISION OF AN ADULT.

SEWING IS FUN BUT, AS ALWAYS,
SAFETY COMES FIRST.

This book is an invitation to sew.

No single book can teach you everything there is to know about sewing. There are some things about sewing that you have to discover for yourself. But this book can give you a good start by showing you what some of the possiblities are. Later you can find books about how to sew your own clothes, how to embroider, how to make lovely things for the home, and even how to make toys. To get started, try some of the projects here, see what you enjoy doing, and then try some more. Don't worry that your sewing doesn't look "professional." You don't want it to—that's the whole point. You want people to know that you made these things yourself. They will be amazed, and you will be proud. A gift made by hand is a very special gift and will be treasured always.

FACING PAGE:

The author wearing a flannel kimono

sewn by her mother

BERNICE SAPIRSTEIN DAVIS

to whom this book is dedicated

TABLE OF CONTENTS

TABLE OF CONTENTS

THE SEWING PROJECTS

by ELISE M. WOLLENWEBER

GETTING READY TO SEW

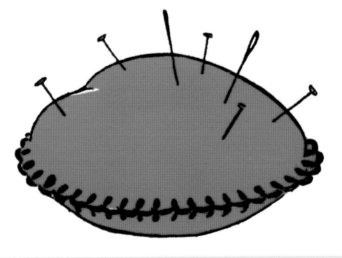

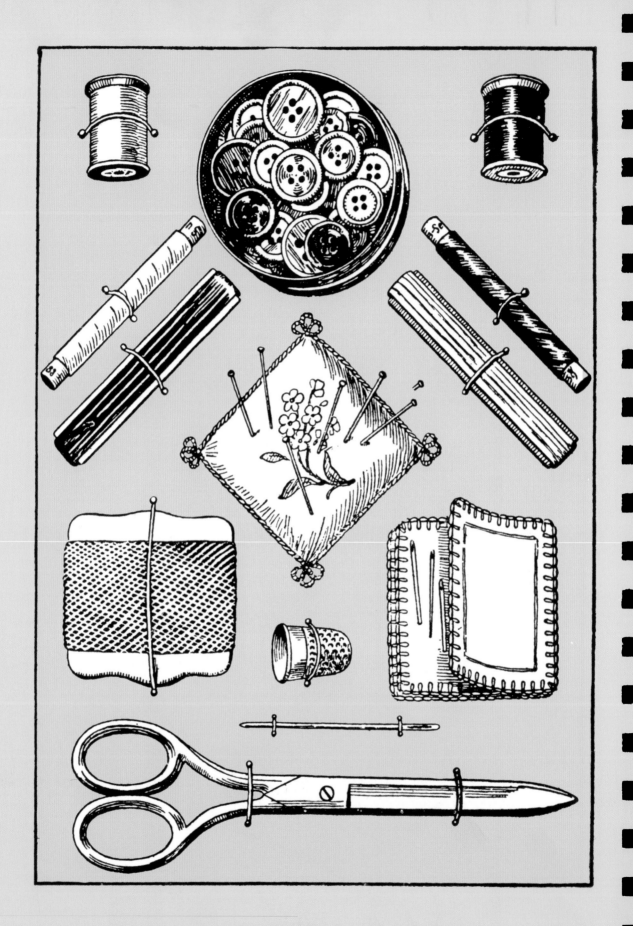

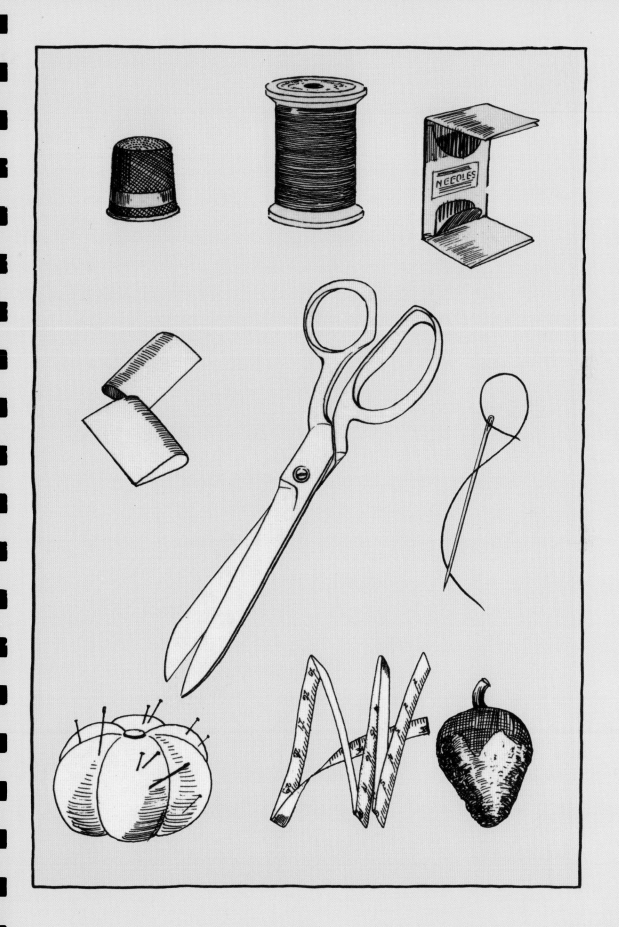

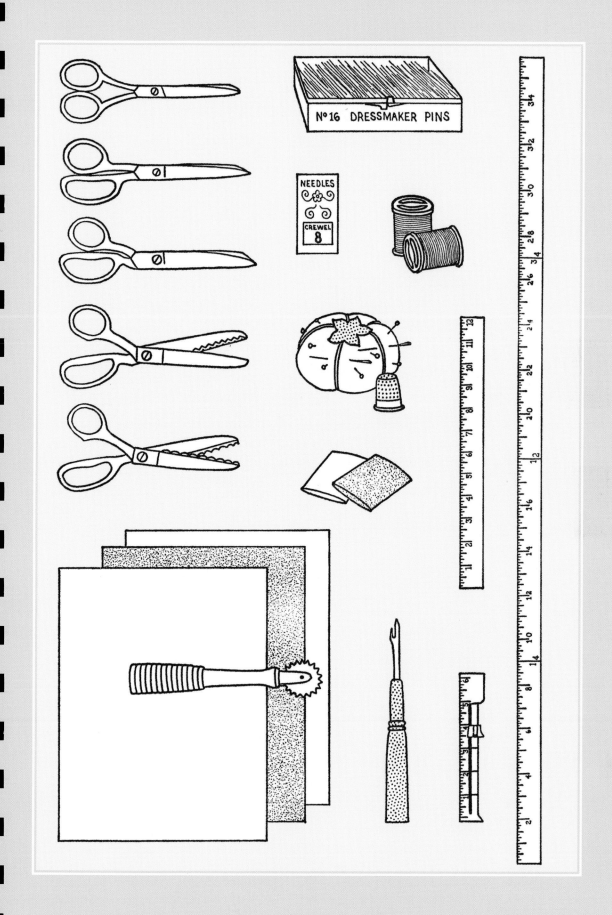

MAKING A SEWING BASKET

Before you begin to sew, you need to assemble a sewing basket (or box) and fill it with all the tools you will need. When you feel like sewing or when you have a sewing emergency—usually a loose button—you will have everything at hand.

BASKET OR BOX WITH A LID: *Find a pretty basket or box with a lid. Make sure it is big enough to hold everything you have, and has some extra room for things you might add later. You will save a lot of time if you have all the items you need at hand.*

THREAD: *Thread comes in different thicknesses and different fibers. You will always want to have several spools of all-purpose thread, in basic colors, on hand. You may also want to have button thread. This is heavier than all-purpose thread and is used for sewing buttons that get a lot of use—as on a coat. Many of the projects in this book use craft thread. This is a thick but soft thread that comes in many colors. It is used when the stitches are meant to be seen. See page 23 to find out more about thread.*

NEEDLES: *Needles come in many sizes. Which one you use depends on the fabric, thread, and kind of sewing you are doing. There are special needles for embroidery and cross stitch. Needles are usually sold in packages containing many different sizes. See pages 28 and 36 to find out more about needles.*

SCISSORS: *Scissors are for cutting fabric and thread. They should be of good quality and comfortable to hold. You may want two pair: a large pair for cutting fabric and a smaller pair for cutting thread and for trimming. Pinking shears are scissors that cut a zig-zag edge that doesn't unravel. Scissors will stay sharp if you use them only to cut fabric and thread and not for other household tasks.*

STRAIGHT PINS: *Straight pins hold fabric together while you sew. Straight pins come in different sizes but are usually sold in an all-purpose size. They also come with glass heads, making them easier to handle and to find if you drop them.*

PIN CUSHION: *You will need somewhere safe to put the pins when you're not using them. Making your own pin cushion can be one of your first projects. I like to use two pin cushions, one for pins and one just for needles. There are directions for making a frog pin cushion on page 87. Do you know why pin cushions are often made to look like tomatoes? Putting a tomato on the mantle of your fireplace was supposed to keep away evil spirts and bring good luck. If a fresh tomato was not available, one was made out of red fabric.*

PENCIL/TAILOR'S CHALK: *Sometimes you will need to mark your fabric. You will want to use a pencil with soft lead so that it can be easily brushed off. On dark fabrics you will need a white pencil or tailor's chalk. This chalk is like a big, soft, waxy crayon made just for sewing. It comes in white and other basic colors.*

TAPE MEASURE/RULER: *You will need a ruler and a tape measure. Which you use depends on what you are measuring.*

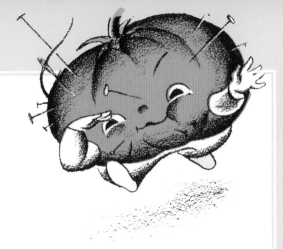

BUTTONS: *Start collecting spare buttons so that if you lose one, you can easily find a replacement. Clothes are often sold with extra buttons. Keep these in your sewing basket.*

IRON AND IRONING BOARD: *Ironing is an important part of sewing. As you finish each stage of your project you will want to press it. This helps keep the project neat and allows you to see how the work you've done is progressing. Pressing can even make imperfect sewing look better. You will also want to iron your project when you have finished. Have an adult help you with this. Irons are very hot.*

THIMBLES: *If you do a lot of sewing, especially a lot of repetitive stitches, you may want to try and use a thimble. You use a thimble to push the needle through the fabric instead of your bare finger. It keeps your fingers from getting sore so you can work more quickly and without discomfort. A thimble is worn on the middle finger of the hand you use for sewing. See page 29 for how to use a thimble.*

Three little mice, with dainty tread,
Set out one day to spin some thread.
"Squeak! squeak!" cried each mouse,
And woke the pussy who slept in the
    house.
"Miaow!" cried she. "May I come
    in?"
And frightened the mice half out of
    their skin!

ALL ABOUT THREAD

Thread can be made from cotton, silk, linen, wool, and many other fibers. Single strands of fiber are twisted together to form thread. This gives the thread strength and flexibility. Thread for general use is made from three strands of fiber. Heavy-duty thread (button thread and craft thread) can have as many as six strands.

There is a thread for every sewing task. There are many threads for general use, mostly used to sew clothing. Heavy-duty button thread is for sewing buttons. It is thicker and stronger than ordinary thread. Embroidery and craft thread come in many different weights and colors depending on the thickness of the fabric you are working on. Many of the projects in this book use a heavy-duty or craft thread. It is easier to work with and will look better.

Always use scissors to cut thread. Do not break or bite it with your teeth. You can easily chip your teeth and the raggedy end will make it more difficult to thread the needle. Thread the needle with the end of the thread that was nearest the spool.

Always use thread one shade darker than your fabric. Thread appears lighter when stitched.

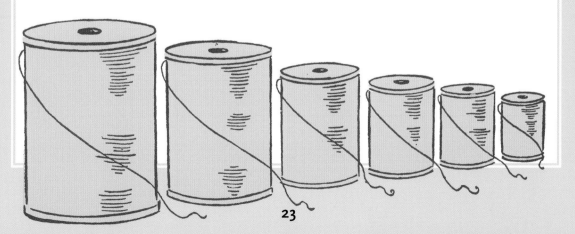

WOOL

POLAR
FLEECE

COTTON

SILK

FELT

LINEN

ALL ABOUT FABRIC

Fabric is thread woven on a loom. The lengthwise threads are called the warp. These threads have to be strong because they carry the weight of the threads that cross them. The threads that cross the warp, side to side, are called the woof. The side edges of the fabric where the cross threads turn are called the selvage.

See if you can find samples of the different fabrics mentioned on the facing page. When you find them, glue a swatch to each box as a reminder.

WOOL: *Wool comes mostly from sheep, but it can also come from other animal coats such as llamas and goats. Wool fibers have a curly shape, creating pockets that trap air. This is called insulation. Insulation gives wool its spongy texture. This is why we use wool to make clothes for cold weather. Wool can absorb 30 percent of its own weight in moisture before it feels damp. Wool can be cooler to wear than polyester because it breathes. Wool is dirt-resistant, flame-resistant, and resists wear and tear. Wool becomes weaker when it is wet.*

COTTON: *The world uses cotton more than any other fiber. Cotton fibers come from the seed pod of the cotton plant. The cotton fiber is hollow in the middle, like a straw, and it is curly, like a ribbon. It is a very versatile fiber. It can be woven into very delicate or very heavy cloth. Cotton can absorb 25 times its weight in water. It also releases water easily (our perspiration) and therefore dries quickly. This is why we wear cotton in hot weather. Cotton is stronger wet than dry.*

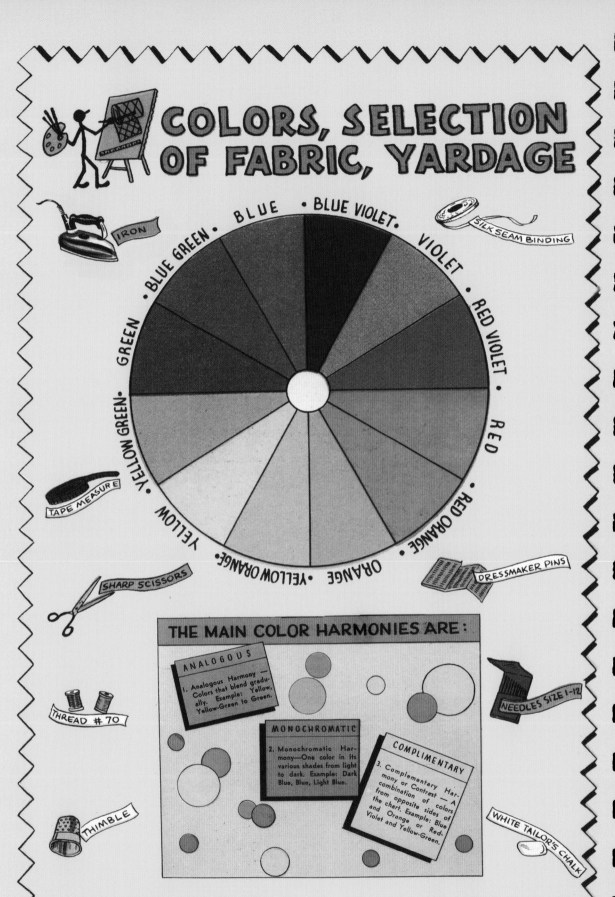

COLORS, SELECTION OF FABRIC, YARDAGE

IRON

SILK SEAM BINDING

BLUE VIOLET
BLUE
BLUE GREEN
VIOLET
GREEN
RED VIOLET
YELLOW GREEN
RED
TAPE MEASURE
RED ORANGE
YELLOW
ORANGE
YELLOW ORANGE

SHARP SCISSORS

DRESSMAKER PINS

THREAD # 70

NEEDLES SIZE 1-12

THIMBLE

WHITE TAILOR'S CHALK

THE MAIN COLOR HARMONIES ARE:

ANALOGOUS

1. Analogous Harmony — Colors that blend gradually. Example: Yellow, Yellow-Green to Green.

MONOCHROMATIC

2. Monochromatic Harmony—One color in its various shades from light to dark. Example: Dark Blue, Blue, Light Blue.

COMPLIMENTARY

3. Complementary Harmony or Contrast — A combination of colors from opposite sides of the chart. Example: Blue and Orange or Red-Violet and Yellow-Green.

FELT: *Felt is a wonderful fabric to use when you are learning to sew. Many of the projects in this book can be made with felt. It is not woven. The fibers are pressed together with heat. It is strong, it can be easily cut, and the edges do not fray. Wool felt is stronger and softer than synthetic felt.*

POLAR FLEECE: *This fabric is made from 100 percent recycled polyester. Polar fleece is the new felt. Like felt, it is easy to sew with, easily cut, and its edges do not fray. Unlike felt, it comes in many different weights. It is hypoallergenic, does not shrink, and the colors do not fade. That's why it is used so often for sport clothing.*

SILK: *Silk is one of the oldest fibers known to man. The fibers come from the cocoon of the silkworm. Silk is the strongest natural fiber. That's why it was used for parachutes before the invention of synthetic fibers. Silk absorbs moisture easily and dries quickly. It is cool in summer and warm in winter. It is very costly to gather a lot of silk threads. This is why silk is considered a luxury fabric. Unlike cotton and wool, silk does not shrink.*

LINEN: *Linen fibers come from the stalk of the flax plant. Linen is the strongest of the vegetable fibers. It is twice as strong as cotton. It contains a natural wax which is why it has a luster when you iron it. It is highly absorbent and dries quickly. That's why linen stays cool in hot weather. Linen is lint-free, making it a good choice for table cloths and napkins. Also, it does not fade.*

ALL ABOUT NEEDLES

Needles come in many sizes. Which one you use depends on the weight of the fabric and the thread you are sewing with. The most common type of needles are called "sharps." There are also special needles for embroidery and darning. You can determine which needle to use by putting the needle through the fabric. If the needle passes through the fabric with difficulty and leaves a hole, it is too big. If the needle slips through too easily with no pushing, then the needle is too small. When you are learning to sew, you will find a big needle is much easier to use than a small one.

HOW TO USE A THIMBLE

Thimbles are for protection and speed. Thimbles are worn on the middle finger of the hand you use for sewing. They come in different sizes and should fit on your finger comfortably. You push the top of the thimble against the top of the needle. It may take some getting used to, but it will help your sewing.

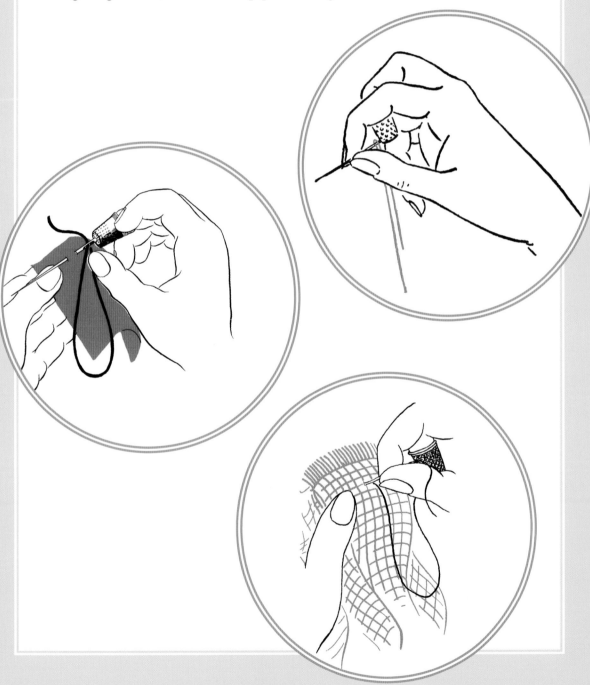

ALL ABOUT PRESSING

Learning how to press and when to press is an important part of sewing. Get in the habit of pressing as you sew. Pressing your project at every stage will improve the look of your sewing and will help you to sew better. You will be able to see more clearly what you have done and what needs to be done. Felt and polar fleece do not need to be, nor should they be, pressed.

Pressing is not ironing. Pressing is just what it says, you simply press the seam with the tip of the iron. You don't use a back and forth motion; it's more a lower and lift motion. Use an iron with a steam setting. The steam provides moisture which helps set the seams.

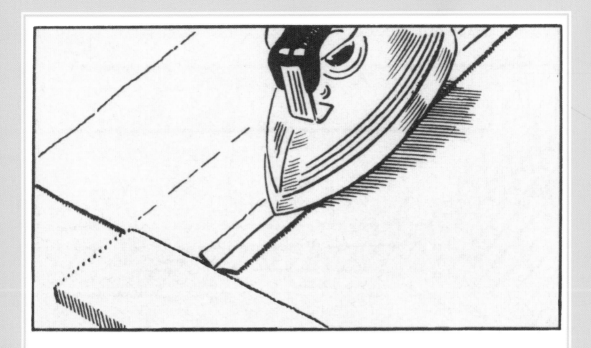

Before you start, test your fabric to make sure the level of heat is correct. This is most important when using synthetic fabrics which can burn or even melt!

Pressing is always done on the wrong side (not the side that will show) of the fabric.

Remove all pins before ironing. Pressing over pins will scratch the surface of the iron.

Make sure your hands are dry when using an iron. Never operate any electrical appliance with wet hands. Do not iron near water.

Irons are very hot. Always ask an adult to help you.

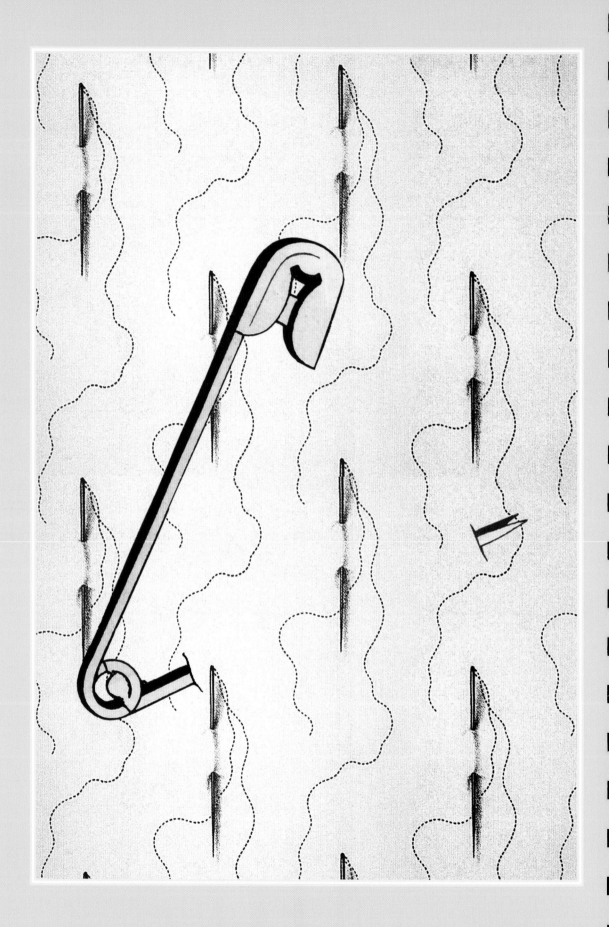

SEWING SAFELY

1 Sit in a comfortable chair in which you can sit up straight. You should have plenty of room in front of you to work. Your arms should be free to move. You can also work at a table.

2 Always sew in a well-lighted room. Sewing near a window with daylight is best and very pleasant. If you need glasses, be sure to wear them. If you have to strain your eyes to see you will get tired quickly.

3 Use a pin cushion to hold your pins and needles. Never hold pins by putting them in your mouth. If you drop a lot of pins on the floor, use a magnet to help you pick them up.

4 Never use your teeth to break thread. Always use a scissors. The end of a thread that has been cleanly cut with a scissors will be easier to put through the eye of the needle. You don't want to risk chipping your teeth.

5 When not in use, keep the scissors in your sewing basket with the points closed. When handing anyone a pair of scissors, make sure the points are closed and are pointing towards you, not the person you are handing them to.

6 Have an adult assist you when you use an iron. Irons get very hot. When not pressing, do not rest the iron on your fabric. Always make sure your hands are dry when using the iron or any electrical appliance. Do not iron near water.

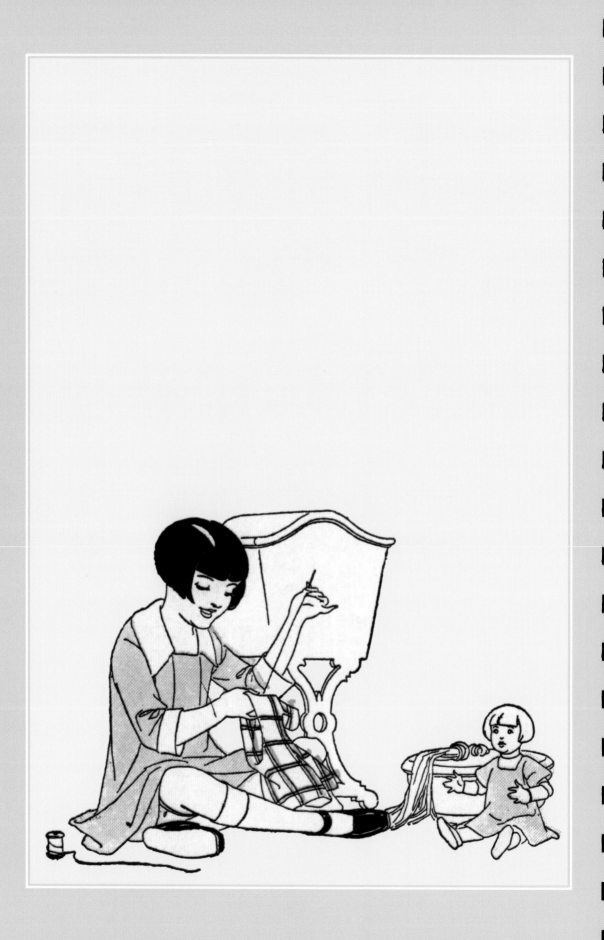

HOW TO BEGIN

HOW TO THREAD A NEEDLE

1. *Cut a piece of thread the length of your arm. If the thread is too long, it will tangle and make sewing difficult.*

2. *Use scissors to cut the thread. Do not use your teeth. It's not good for your teeth and a ragged end will be harder to thread through the eye of the needle.*

3. *The thread is less likely to tangle if you put the end that was closer to the spool through the eye of the needle.*

4. *Hold one hand against the other to keep your hands steady.*

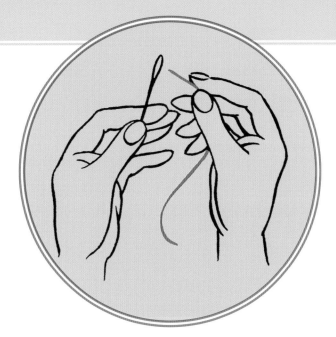

5 *Hold the needle and thread against something white or near a bright light to see it better.*

6 *Hold the needle in your left hand, and hold the end of the thread in your right hand (opposite if you are left-handed). Push the end of the thread through the eye of the needle. You may want to wet the end of the thread if you are having difficulty getting it through.*

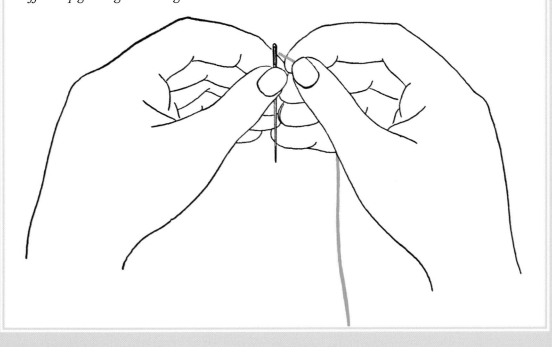

HOW TO MAKE A KNOT

1 Hold the end of the thread between your thumb and index finger.

2 Wind the long end around the tip of your index finger and hold it with your thumb.

3 Slide your thumb forward along your index finger, twisting the thread together as you slide.

4 When the twist comes off your finger, pull down toward the end to make a knot. It may sound difficult, but if you look at the pictures on the opposite page you will see how easy it is. You may have to practice a few times. Watching someone who knows how to make a knot is the easiest way to learn. The knot doesn't have to be big, but it has to be big enough not to come through the weave of the fabric.

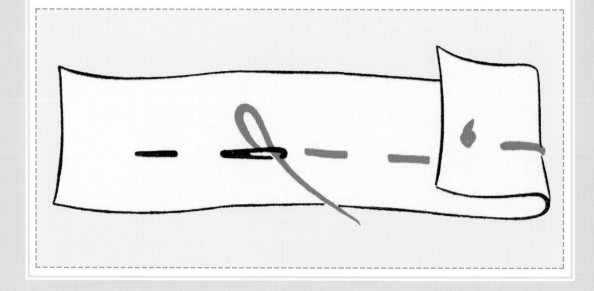

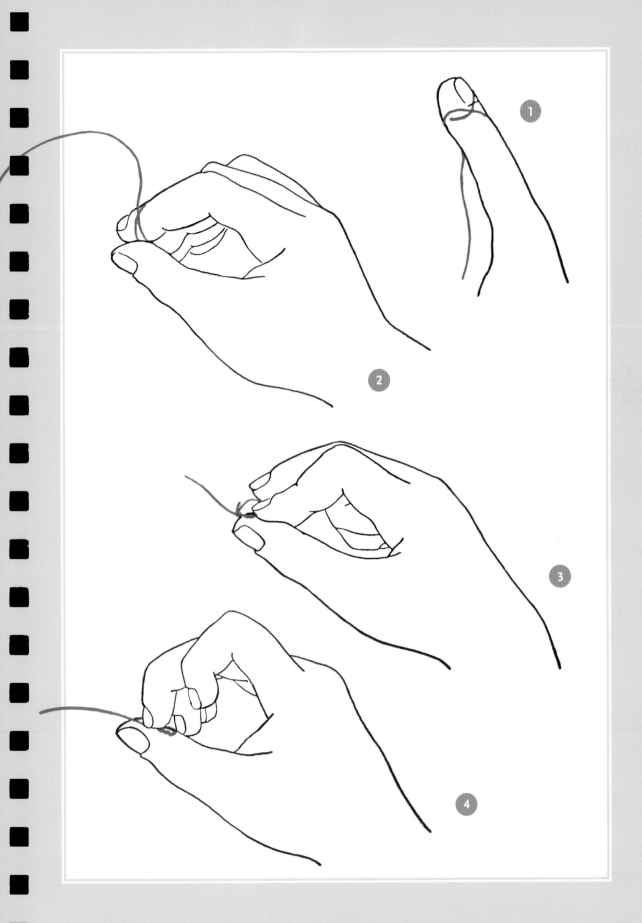

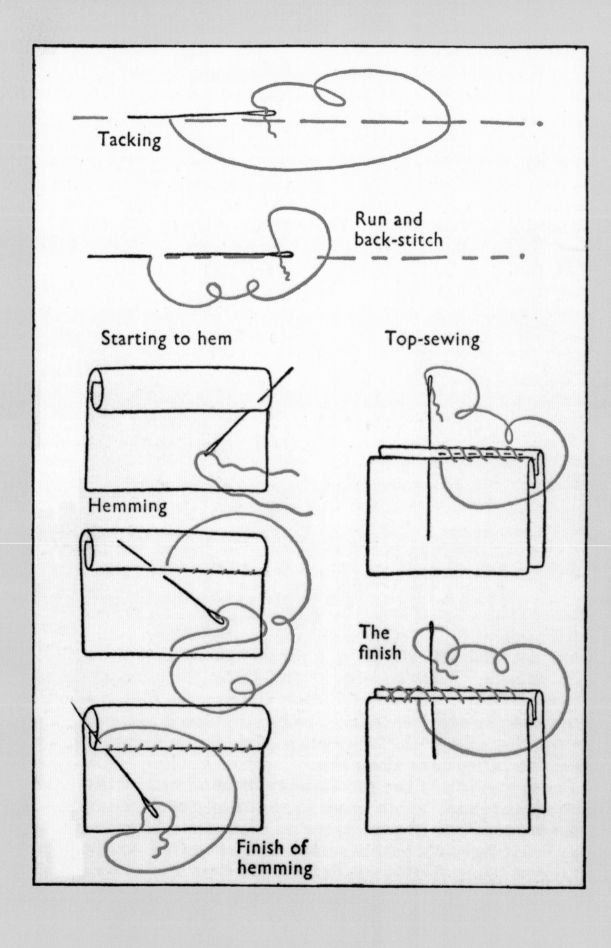

Tacking

Run and back-stitch

Starting to hem

Top-sewing

Hemming

The finish

Finish of hemming

BASIC SEWING STITCHES

BASTING STITCH

Basting is used to hold the fabric in place while you sew. Basting is not permanent and is removed after you've sewn the permanent stitches. The basting stitch is larger and looser than permanent stitches. Use a different color thread for the basting so that you can easily tell which stitches are the basting. Basting may seem like an unnecessary step but it will hold your fabric perfectly in place. If you only pin the fabric, it can slip. Also, if you only use pins, they may stick you as you sew.

TO BASTE: *Thread the needle and make a knot. Pin the pieces of fabric together and begin about ¼" away from where the permanent stitching will go, bringing the needle and thread up through the fabric at* Ⓐ *then down through the fabric again at* Ⓑ *to make each stitch. Make the stitches about ¼ to ½" long. When you have finished, make a knot as close to the fabric as possible, then cut the thread about 1" from the knot. The 1" tail will make it easier to pull out the thread.*

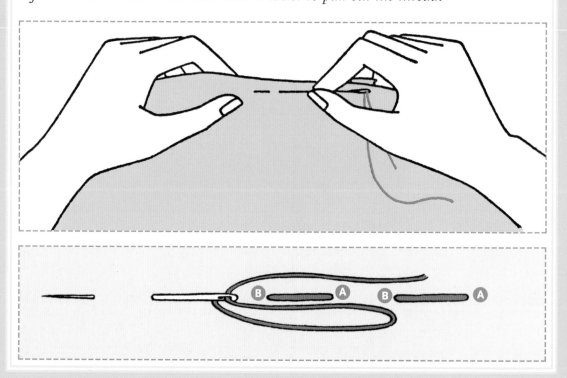

RUNNING STITCH

The running stitch is the most basic and most often-used stitch. This is the stitch you will use for many of the projects in this book. The stitches should be small and of even length. The thread should not be pulled too tightly or too loosely. The size of the stitches depends on the weight of the fabric and thread. When the fabric is turned inside out, the stitches should be almost invisible.

RUNNING STITCH: *Thread the needle and make a knot. Begin sewing at either edge. When you reach the end of the seam, make a knot and cut the thread close to the knot. The running stitch is the same as the basting stitch but the stitches are closer together and you can do more than one stitch at a time.*

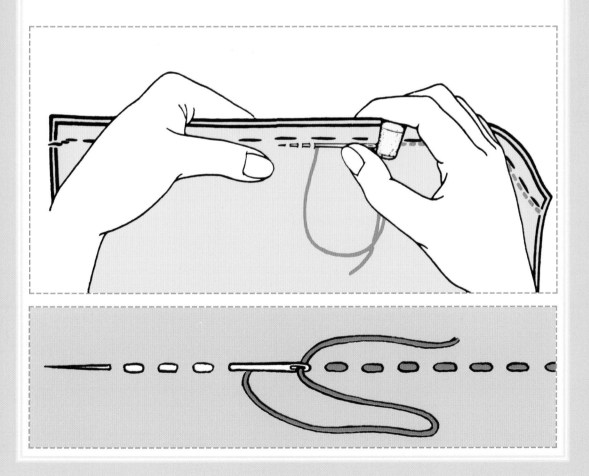

BACKSTITCH

The backstitch is used when you need a very strong seam.

BACKSTITCH: *Begin as for a running stitch at* Ⓐ *. Instead of starting the next stitch ahead, go back to the end of the last stitch* Ⓑ *. Begin the next stitch by coming up through the fabric at* Ⓒ *. Instead of space between each stitch as with the running stitch, the stitches will touch, end to end.*

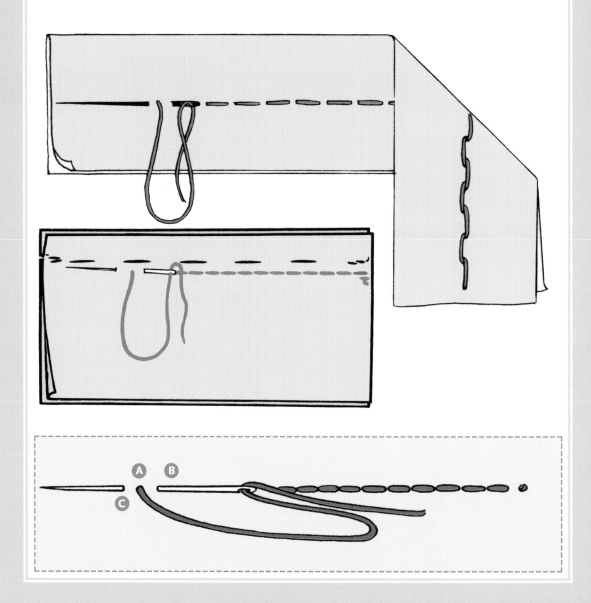

GATHERING

Gathers are made with a loosely sewn running stitch (see page 43).

GATHERING: *After the stitches are sewn, the thread is pulled to create a gather. To hold the gathers while you adjust the fabric, wind the thread around a pin in a figure 8, as shown in the bottom illustration. When you have the gathers just as you want them, unwind the thread and make a knot.*

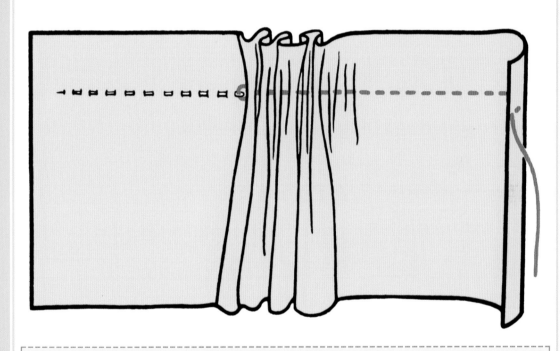

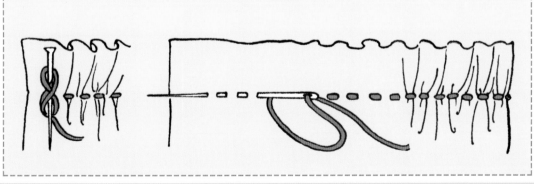

HEMMING

To make a hem, the fabric is folded down twice to "hide" the raw edge. The folded edge is sewn to the fabric. Hemming is done on the wrong side of the fabric.

HEMMING: *Fold the fabric twice as shown below. Pin, then baste. Remove pins. Thread your needle and make a knot at one end. Hide the knot under the hem edge where you start. Using the point of the needle and keeping the needle at a slant, make a small stitch picking up two or three threads at* A *. Then come up from the back catching the edge of the fold at* B *. If the stitches are too big they will show through to the other side. If they are too small the folded hem will tear away from the fabric the first time you wash it.*

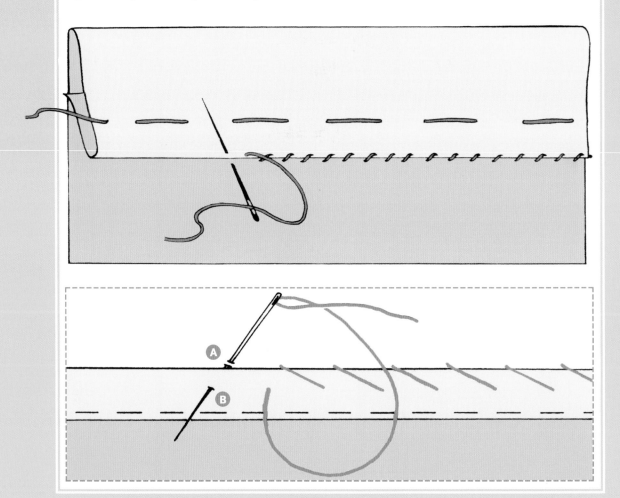

SLIP STITCH

The slip stitch is an invisible stitch. It is used for hemming or holding trims in place. It is not a strong stitch.

SLIP STITCH: *Baste fabric as described on page 42. Remove pins. Insert the threaded needle into the folded edge. Using a small stitch pick up one or two threads on the underside of the folded fabric. Then pick up one or two threads on the fabric below. Do not pull too tightly. Remove basting after slip stitch is sewn.*

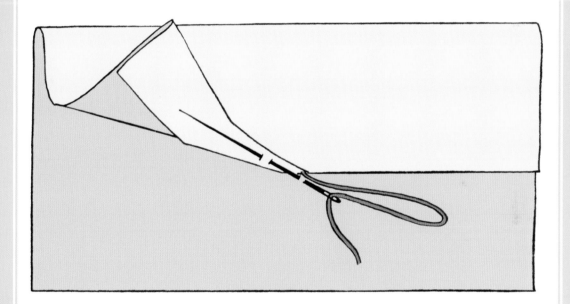

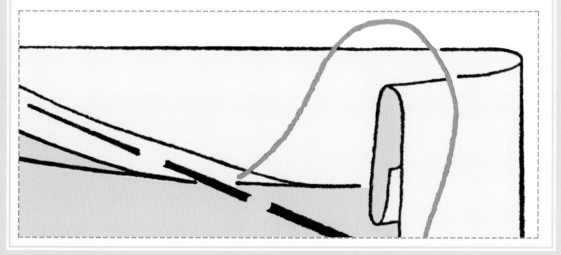

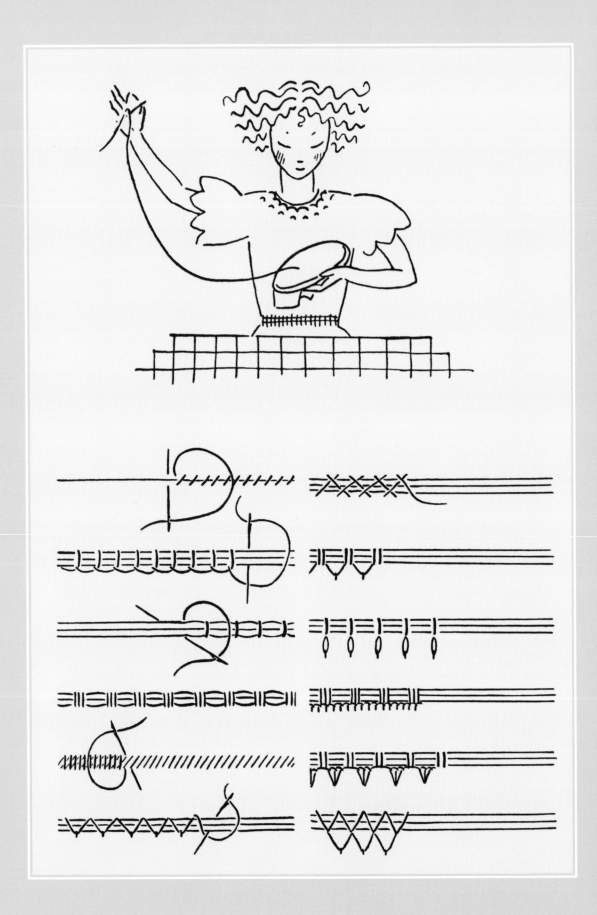

BASIC EMBROIDERY STITCHES

CHAIN STITCH

CHAIN STITCH: *This stitch makes a line of loops. Bring the needle up through the fabric at* A *. Hold the thread under the thumb of the hand that is holding the fabric. Now push the needle down through the same hole to the back of the fabric. Still holding the loop, bring the needle up again at* B *and pull firmly to form the first loop. Hold the thread under your thumb and make another loop as above.*

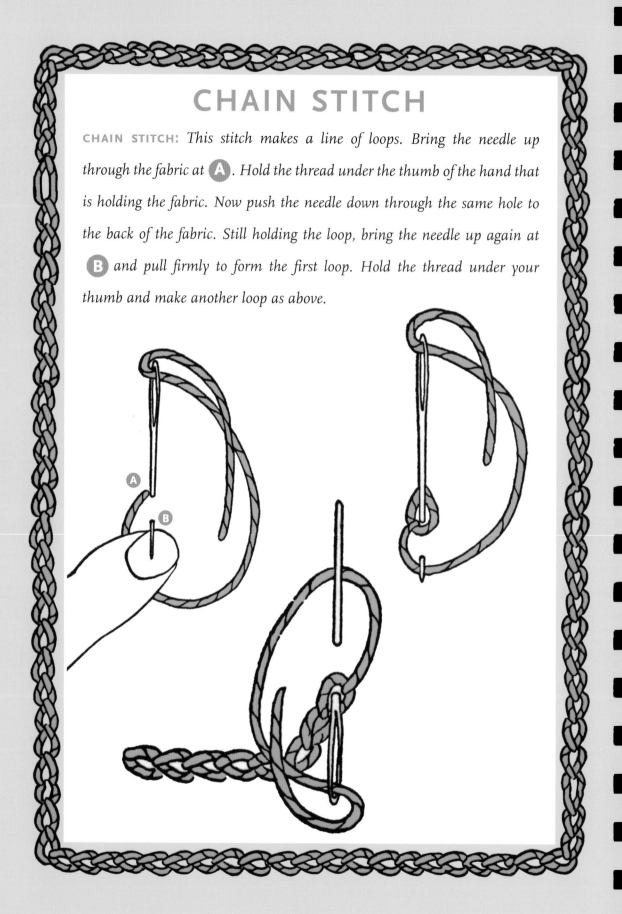

STEM STITCH

STEM STITCH: *This stitch is used for outlining or filling in a design. The stitches are sewn at a slant. Bring the needle up through the back of the fabric at* **A**. *Put the needle down through the fabric about ½" away at* **B**. *Bring the needle back up about halfway in front of the first stitch at* **C**. *Continue making stitches in front of the last stitch you have sewn as in the illustrations below.*

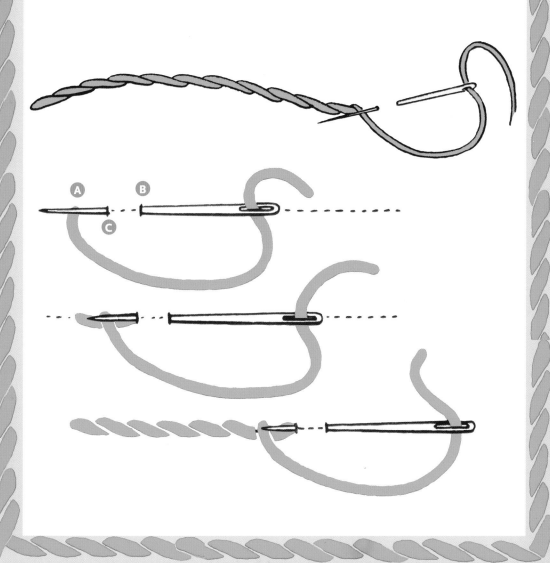

FRENCH KNOTS

FRENCH KNOTS: *This stitch makes a raised dot. It is used for filling in, like the center of a flower, or used singly, like the eyes on the sock doll on page 97. You can vary the size of the knot by using different weights of thread or varying the number of times you wrap the thread around the needle.*

Bring the threaded needle up through the fabric. Hold the thread with your left thumb and forefinger. Holding the needle in your right hand, wind the thread around the needle once or twice, depending on the size of the knot you want. While still holding the thread in your left hand, insert the needle back into the fabric, very near the point where you began. Use the index finger of your left hand to hold the knot down while you finish pulling the thread through the back. For a larger knot, it is better to use heavier thread than to wind the needle more than twice.

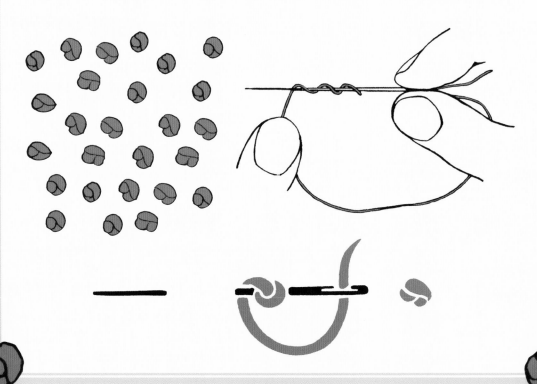

BLANKET STITCH

BLANKET STITCH: *This stitch is used for finishing edges as well as decoration. If you vary the spacing of the stitches you can make all kinds of designs. Bring the needle up through the fabric very close to the edge at* **A**. *This will secure the thread to the fabric. Push the needle down through the fabric on the right side ¼ to ½" from the edge at* **B**. *Keep the thread loose. Now bring the point of the needle through the loop at* **C**. *Push the needle down again, the same distance from the edge as before and continue in the same manner.*

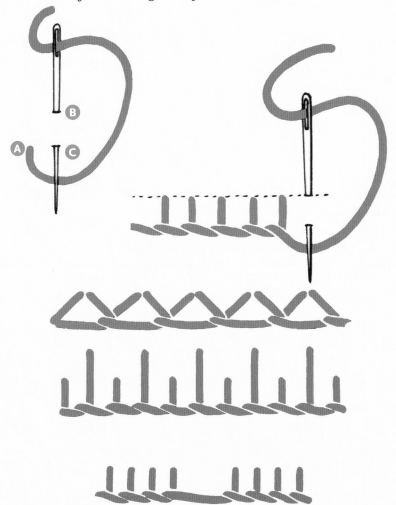

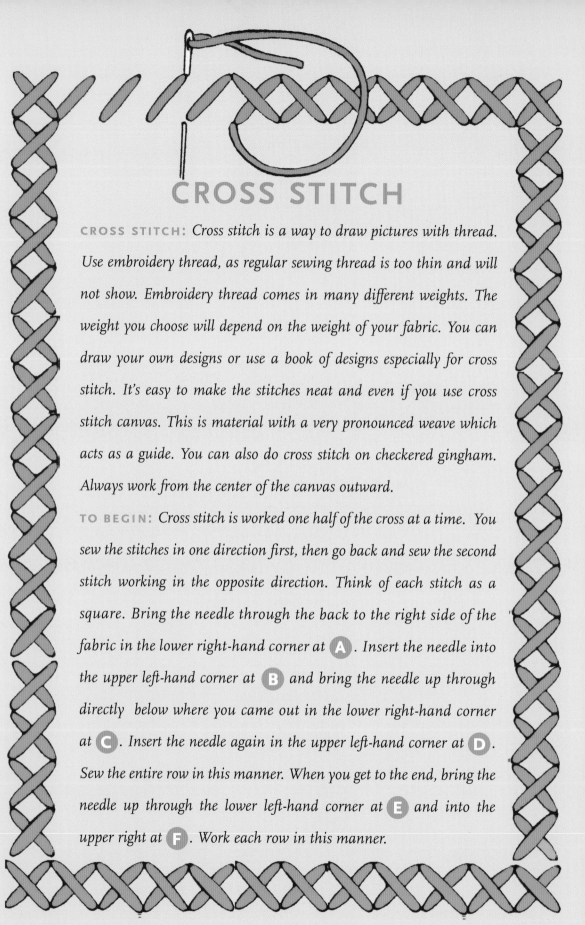

CROSS STITCH

CROSS STITCH: *Cross stitch is a way to draw pictures with thread. Use embroidery thread, as regular sewing thread is too thin and will not show. Embroidery thread comes in many different weights. The weight you choose will depend on the weight of your fabric. You can draw your own designs or use a book of designs especially for cross stitch. It's easy to make the stitches neat and even if you use cross stitch canvas. This is material with a very pronounced weave which acts as a guide. You can also do cross stitch on checkered gingham. Always work from the center of the canvas outward.*

TO BEGIN: *Cross stitch is worked one half of the cross at a time. You sew the stitches in one direction first, then go back and sew the second stitch working in the opposite direction. Think of each stitch as a square. Bring the needle through the back to the right side of the fabric in the lower right-hand corner at* **A**. *Insert the needle into the upper left-hand corner at* **B** *and bring the needle up through directly below where you came out in the lower right-hand corner at* **C**. *Insert the needle again in the upper left-hand corner at* **D**. *Sew the entire row in this manner. When you get to the end, bring the needle up through the lower left-hand corner at* **E** *and into the upper right at* **F**. *Work each row in this manner.*

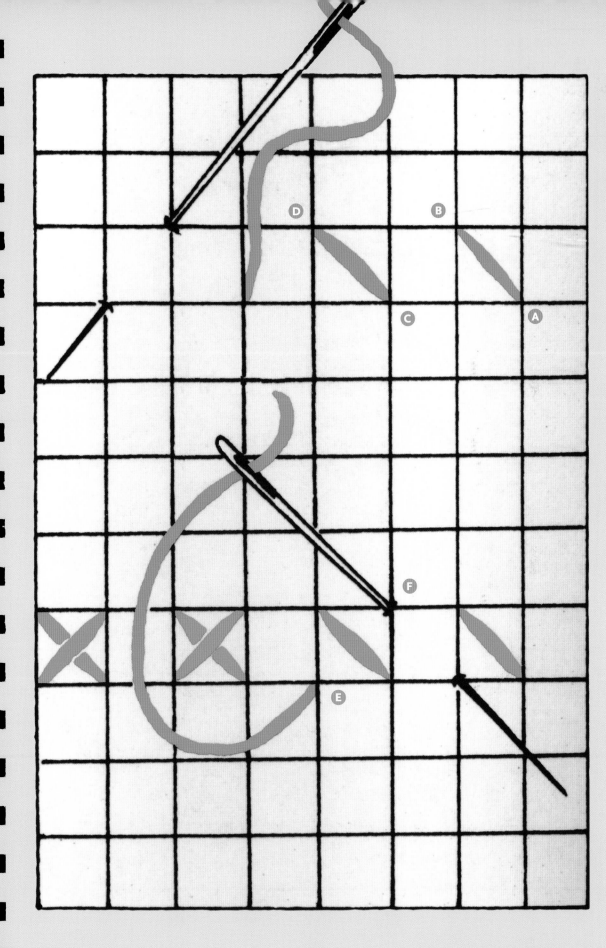

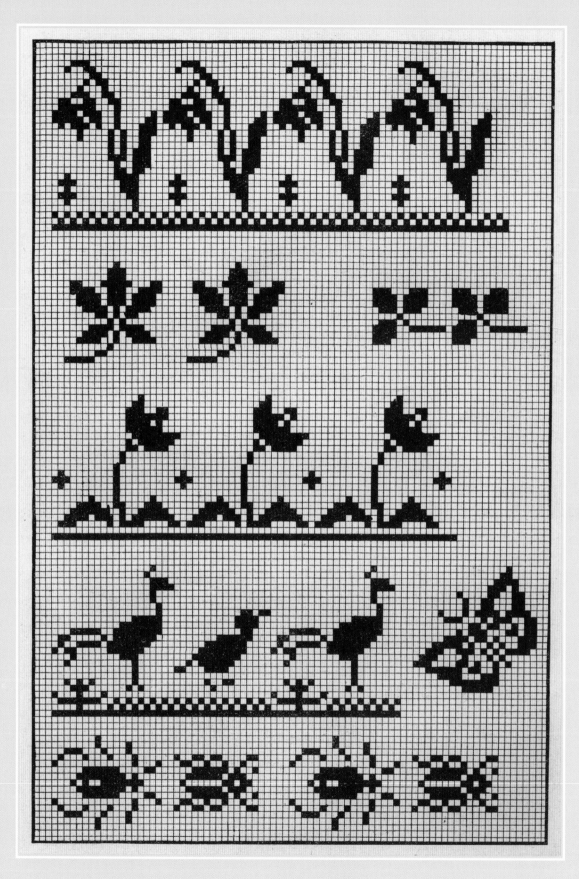

PINK
BLUE
RED
GOLD

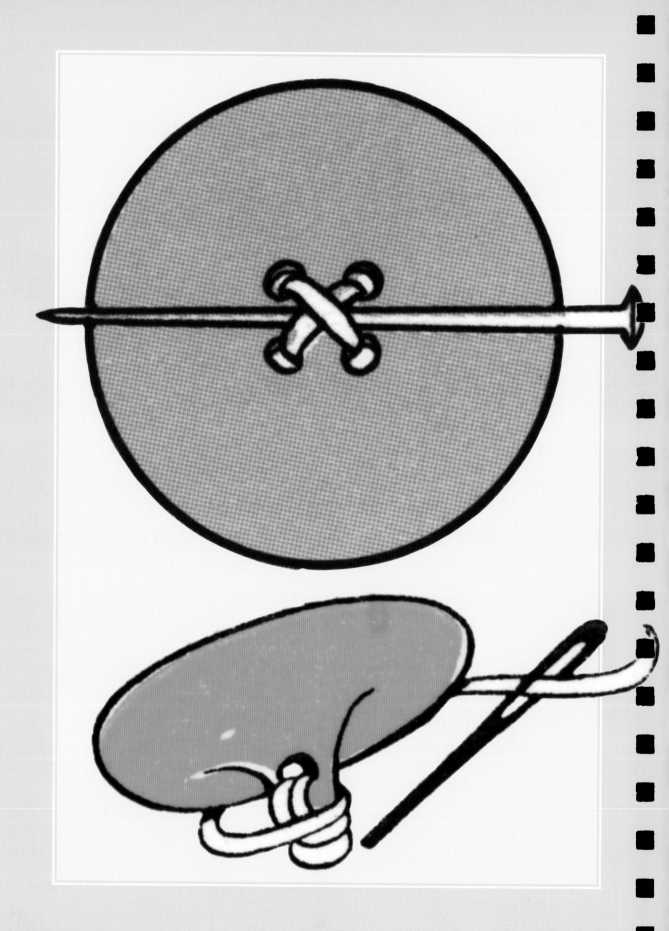

HOW TO
SEW ON
A BUTTON

HOLE BUTTONS

This is the most common type of button. When you sew a hole button, you have to create a shank or stem to make room between the button and the fabric. If you don't, the fabric will not lie smoothly when the garment is buttoned. It also makes it more difficult to pass the button through the hole. If you are attaching a button just for decoration, you don't have to sew a shank.

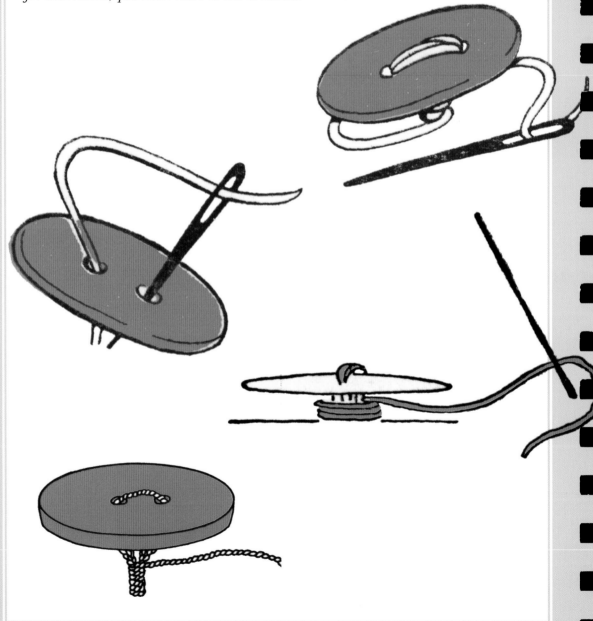

SHANK BUTTONS

These are shank buttons. Shank buttons come with a stem or stitching loop attached to the button. The shank creates a space between the button and the fabric the button is sewn to. If there isn't enough space, the two pieces of fabric will not lie smoothly when buttoned.

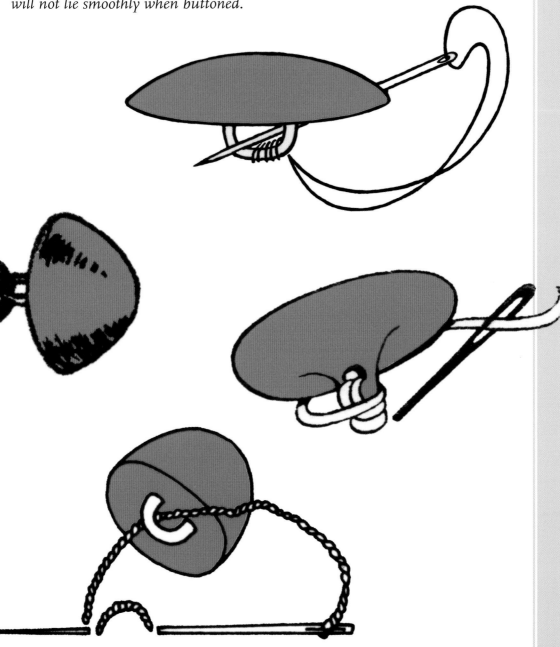

HOW TO SEW
ON A HOLE BUTTON

Thread the needle and make a knot at the long end of the thread (see pages 36–39). On the fabric, mark the spot with a pin where you want to attach the button.

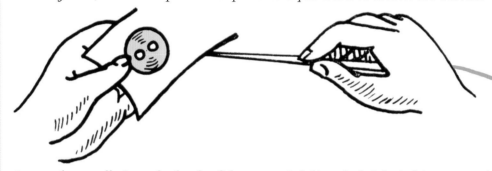

Insert the needle into the back of the material directly behind this spot. Bring the needle and thread upward through the fabric until the knot is snug against the fabric. Bring the needle through the first hole of the button and let the button lie flat against the fabric.

Bring the needle down through the second hole and through the fabric, close to where you came through the first time. Pull the thread snugly, but not too tight. At this point, you need to insert a pin or toothpick under the first stitch. This will help create the "stem" (see page 63).

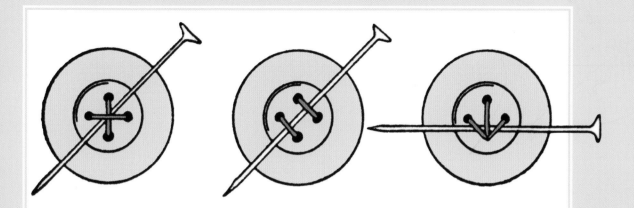

Repeat the steps at left four or five times until the button is firmly sewn. If your button has four holes, work the second set of holes in the same way. When finished, remove the pin or toothpick, pull the button away from the fabric, and wind the thread around the threads between the button and the fabric. Push the needle through to the back of the material close to the stem. Make a knot close to the material and cut with a scissors. Do not pull or break off and never use your teeth!

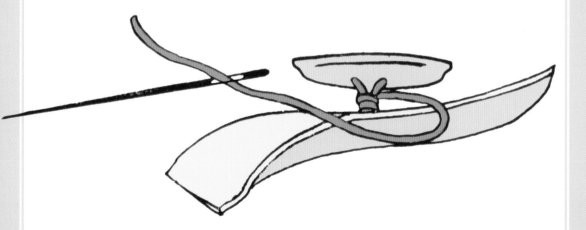

With four holes you can either make an "x" working all four holes at the same time, or you can work two holes at a time (see the illustrations above). Either way, you need to repeat four or five times with each set of holes until the button is sewn firmly, but not too firmly.

HOW TO SEW
ON A SHANK BUTTON

Thread the needle and make a knot(see pages 36-39). Mark the spot where you want to attach the button with a pin.

Insert the needle into the back of the material directly behind where the button will be sewn. Bring the needle and thread upward through the fabric until the knot is snug against the fabric. Bring the needle through the shank of the button. Pull so the shank is snug against the material.

Bring the needle down through the fabric, close to where the shank touches the fabric. Bring the needle up in the same spot where you started. Repeat the above steps four or five times until the button is firmly sewn. When finished, wind the thread around the shank about five times, close to the fabric. Push the needle through to the back of the material. Make a knot close to the material and cut with a scissors. Do not pull or break off and never use your teeth!

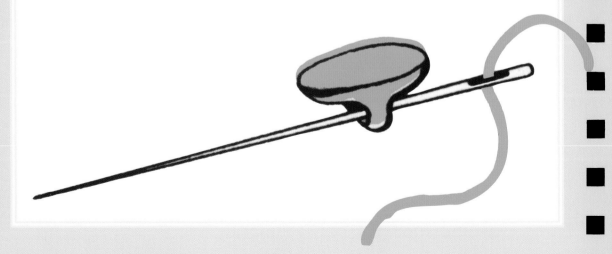

OTHER KINDS OF FASTENERS

HOOKS & EYES: *Hooks and eyes are usually small but also come larger and heavier. Whether small or large, they are very strong. You can use them singly or in a row, as on the front of a jacket. Often they are used at the top of a zipper to keep the flap flat. They come with straight or looped eyes. Which kind you need will depend on how you will use them.*

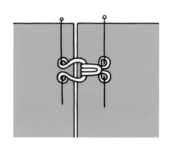

ZIPPERS: *Zippers are made in many lengths, sizes, and colors. They are also made in different materials, usually metal or plastic. The zipper was invented in 1891 by Whitcomb L. Judson of Chicago. In 1894, he and Lewis Walker set up the Universal Fastener Company.*

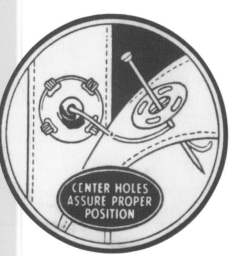

CENTER HOLES ASSURE PROPER POSITION

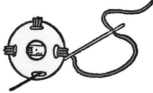

SNAPS: *Snaps are made in pairs. They are sewn on one at a time, but must be positioned with pins so they match. When you finish, the fabric should lie completely flat. If it puckers, remove one of the snaps and sew it on again.*

THE
SEWING
PROJECTS

DRAWSTRING BAG

A drawstring bag is a good first project. It is easily made and very useful. Once you have made the bag using the measurements given here, you will be able to make bags in all different sizes and fabrics depending on your needs. You can use almost any fabric, but keep the use of the bag in mind. If you think you might want to wash the bag later, you should preshrink the fabric before you begin.

MATERIALS: *1 piece of fabric 12 x 24", ½" ribbon or cord 30" long, needle, thread for basting, thread for sewing, tailor's chalk, tape measure, 1 large safety pin.*

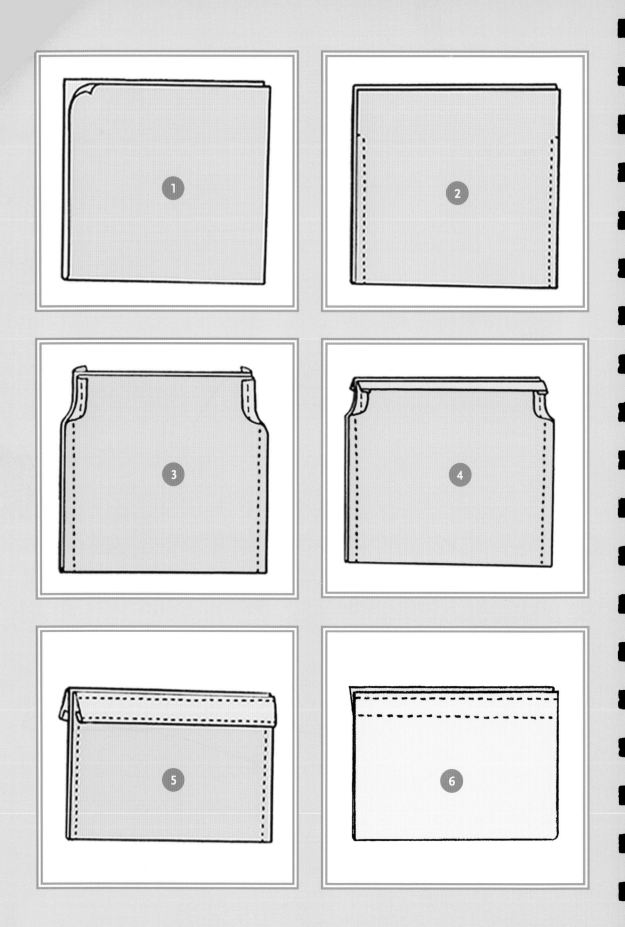

DIRECTIONS: **1** *Fold the fabric in half, right sides together and edges even. The fold will be the bottom of the bag. Pin together. You will be doing all the sewing with the bag inside out. Measure 2½" down from each corner. Mark lightly with a pencil. This indicates where the side openings start.*

2 *Thread the needle with the basting thread and baste each side from the pencil mark to the bottom. Remove pins. Using the backstitch (see page 44), sew the seams on each side from the spot you have marked to the bottom of the bag. The seam should be ¼" in from the edge of the fabric. Remove the basting.*

3 *Lay the bag flat on an ironing surface and press the seams open, including the 2½" above the stitching that wasn't sewn. Baste the 2½". This will hold the fabric in place and out of the way for the next step.*

4 *Still working with the bag inside out, fold down ½" on the top of the side which faces you. Then fold it down again, 1" more. The edge of the fold should just meet the top of the side seams. Pin and then baste the fold. Turn the bag over and repeat on the other side. Remove pins.*

5 *Using the running stitch (see page 43), sew across the lower fold from one edge to the other, ¼" up from the fold. Then sew across again ¼" below the top fold, edge to edge. This will make a casing or tunnel for the ribbon or cord. Turn the bag over and repeat on the other side. Remove the basting from across the bag and from the folded edges. Press the side seams open again and press the casing.*

The directions continue on the next page.

6 *Cut the ribbon in half so you have two equal lengths. Take one piece of the ribbon and attach a 1 or 2" safety pin. Use the safety pin as a guide to pull the ribbon through the casing. After you get the ribbon through and there is an equal amount of ribbon on each side, remove the safety pin. Turn the bag over and repeat on the other side. Match up the ends of the ribbon and knot them together (see the illustration at left and below).*

7 *Turn the bag right side out. Press the two side seams and the bottom fold. Hold each end of the ribbon and gather the bag toward the center. Tie the ribbons in a bow if you wish.*

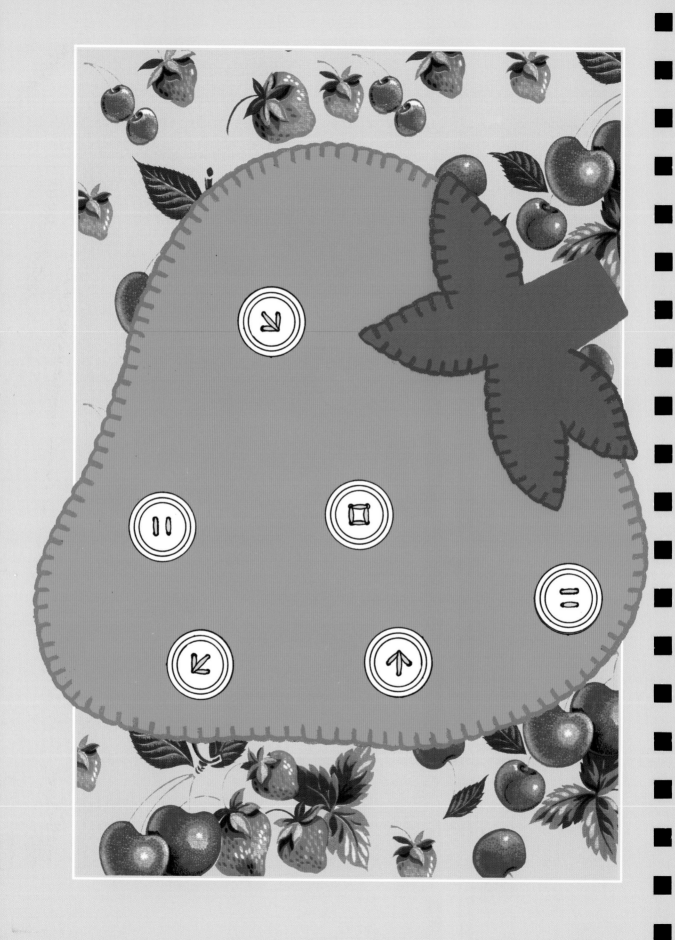

STRAWBERRY POT HOLDER

Pot holders are used to protect your hands from heat. When deciding what kind of fabric to use, think about which combination of materials will give the best protection. Think about which materials will stand up to heavy use and frequent washing. I used old terry cloth towels for the lining. Once you see how easy this Strawberry Pot Holder is, you can make your own patterns in any shape you want.

MATERIALS: *Felt, cotton (not too light-weight), or even an old sweatshirt, button, or craft thread, material for inner lining (terry cloth, cotton batting, sweatshirt), curtain or key ring, small buttons for decoration.*

DIRECTIONS: **1** *Copy the strawberry and stem pattern on page 76 on a copy machine, enlarging if you want a bigger pot holder. Cut out right along the edge. Lay the pattern on the material and pin. Remember you have to cut two strawberries, so make sure you leave enough room to trace the second one. Using a soft pencil or tailor's chalk, trace right around the edge. Remove pattern, turn over and pin to the fabric, and trace again. Cut out both strawberries right along the line. Cut out the stem in the same manner. The stem is already doubled so you only have to cut one.*

2 *Using the same strawberry pattern, trace the strawberry onto the material you are using for the inner lining. Cut this piece ⅛" inside the outline so the lining is smaller than the outside strawberry. If you are going to sew on little buttons for the strawberry's seeds, do that now. It will be much easier and the knots will be completely hidden inside the pot holder. Only sew buttons on one side. You don't want the buttons to interfere with picking up something hot.*

FOLD

3 Lay one strawberry, wrong side facing you, on a flat surface. Place the lining on top, making sure it is centered inside the berry. Lay the second berry on top of the lining with the right side facing you. Match up all the edges. Make sure all three pieces are smooth. Pin together and then baste through all three layers (see page 42). Remove pins.

4 Using the blanket stitch (see page 53), start at Ⓐ and work all around the berry and finish at Ⓑ. Make a knot and trim. Remove basting.

5 Pin, trace, and cut out the stem piece just as you cut out the strawberry. You will only need one since it is doubled for you to fold over. If you want to add a ring to hang the pot holder, you should slip the stem piece through the ring now, before you sew it together.

6 With or without the ring, fold the stem piece in half, matching up the edges of the leaves. Pin together. Using the blanket stitch, stitch the top of leaves together from Ⓒ to Ⓓ. Make a knot. Trim. Thread your needle again (use a longer piece of thread this time) and stitch from Ⓔ to Ⓕ. Do not make a knot. Remove the needle and put in a pin cushion while you place the stem piece on the strawberry. Both sides of the stem piece are the same, so it doesn't matter which side is which. Pin the stem piece in place.

7 Thread the needle again and continue with the blanket stitch all around the edges of the leaves from Ⓒ to Ⓐ. Make a knot and trim. Turn the potholder over and stitch the leaves on the other side to the berry sewing again from Ⓑ to Ⓒ. Make a knot and trim. Tuck tail inside stem.

HOW TO COOK
A SOFT-BOILED EGG

Fill a saucepan with cold water. You can put in as many as four eggs or as few as one as long as the water covers the eggs by one inch. Place over medium-high heat and bring to a boil; lower the heat and simmer for three minutes. Turn off the heat. With a slotted spoon, carefully transfer the eggs to a bowl. Place the bowl in the sink and run cold water over the eggs to stop the cooking. When it is cool enough to handle, place the egg in an egg cup (large end down) and cover with your egg cozy (see page 79). Remove the egg cozy when your toast is done and you are ready to eat.

EGG COZY

An egg cozy is a little cap to keep your soft-boiled egg warm while you are making your toast. You can make it out of any soft fabric, but remember, the fabric should be heavy enough to keep the egg warm. Felt, polar fleece, or a sturdy cotton would be suitable.

MATERIALS: *2 pieces of fabric for the body and wings, at least 5 x 5" each, 1 piece of fabric in a contrasting color for the comb approximately 2" square, needle and thread, 2 beads or small buttons for eyes. The directions begin on the next page.*

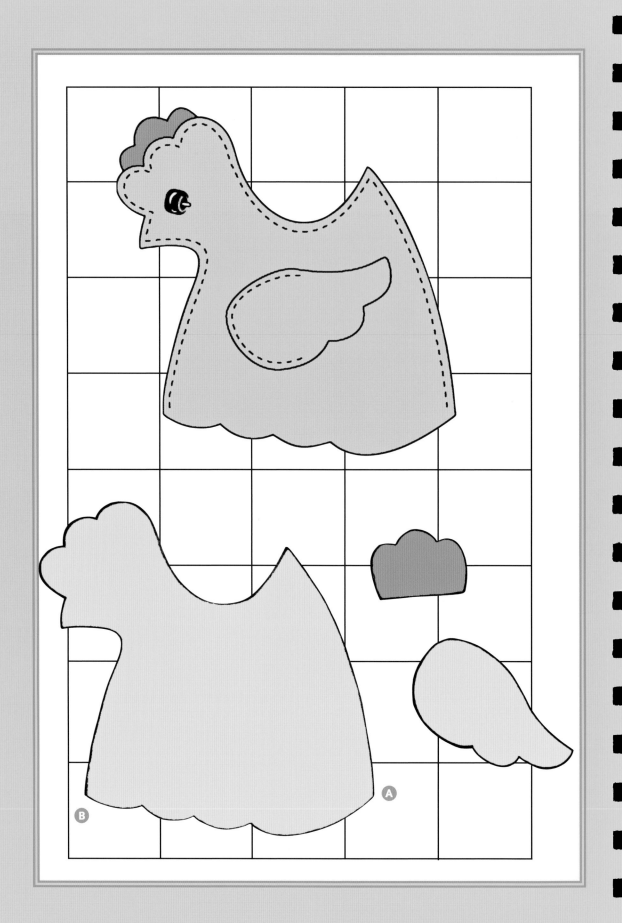

1 *Using a copy machine, make a copy of the pattern on the opposite page.*

2 *Cut out the pattern and trace it onto the material. Cut right on the line. Cut out two chicken bodies, two wings, and one cockscomb.*

3 *If you're going to add wings, you should sew them on now. It will be easier to sew the eyes (buttons, beads, or embroidery) now also.*

4 *With the right sides facing out, hold the two body pieces together. Insert the cockscomb as shown below. Pin, baste (see page 42), then remove pins. Thread the needle and make a knot. At* **A** *start sewing the pieces together using the running stitch (see page 43). When you get to* **B** *make a knot inside so it doesn't show. Remove basting.*

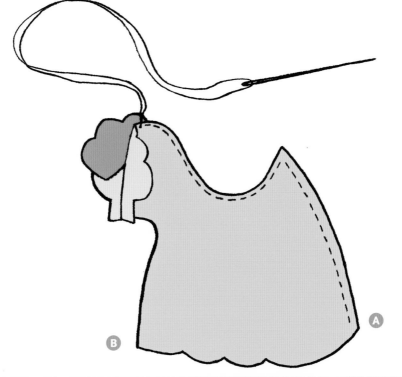

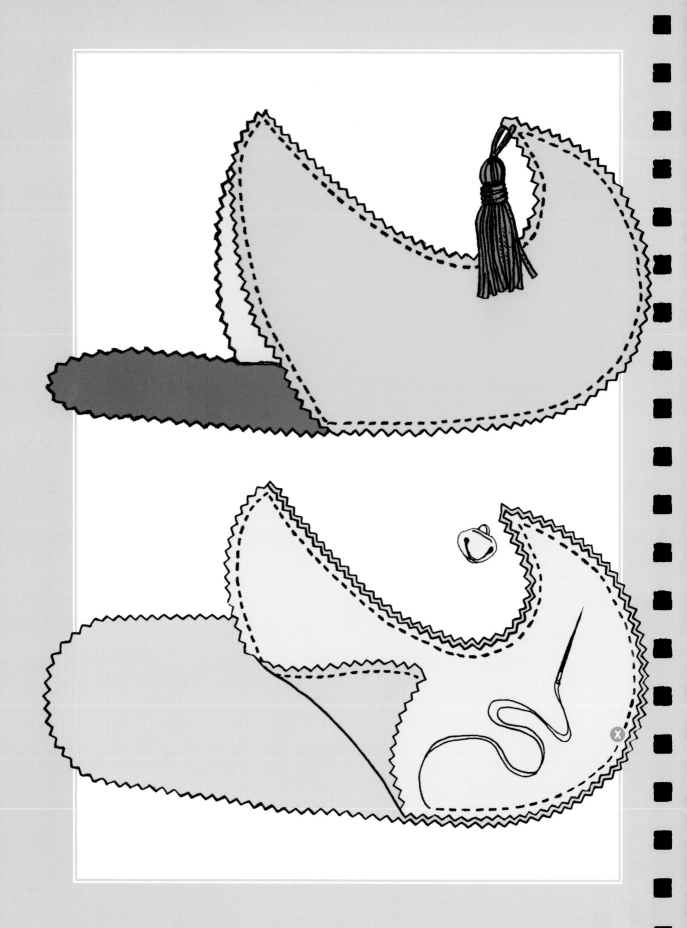

ELF SLIPPERS

These slippers are easy to make and easy to make look wonderful. You can make them out of felt, polar fleece, or even leather! You can make them all one color, or many different colors. You can even use different-colored thread. Be sure to add the non-slip soles on the bottom, as without them they are really very slippery. You don't have to use pinking shears, but I think the pinked edge makes a wonderful decorative element.

MATERIALS: ¼ yard of felt, pinking shears, needle, heavy duty craft or button thread, non-slip soles (you can use non-slip carpet pads), fabric or craft glue, 2 bells (optional).

DIRECTIONS: **1** Copy patterns on a copy machine, enlarging so that patterns are ½" longer than the length of your foot, and cut out. You will need two soles, two non-slip soles, and four side pieces. Pin the patterns to your fabric. Using a soft pencil or tailor's chalk, trace the patterns onto the fabric right along the edge. Remove pins and cut out the pieces. Mark each piece with the **X** that is on the pattern. Cut out the pieces for the non-slip soles ¼" inside the tracing line.

You want the non-slip material to cover most of the sole, but not the stitching.

The directions continue on the next page.

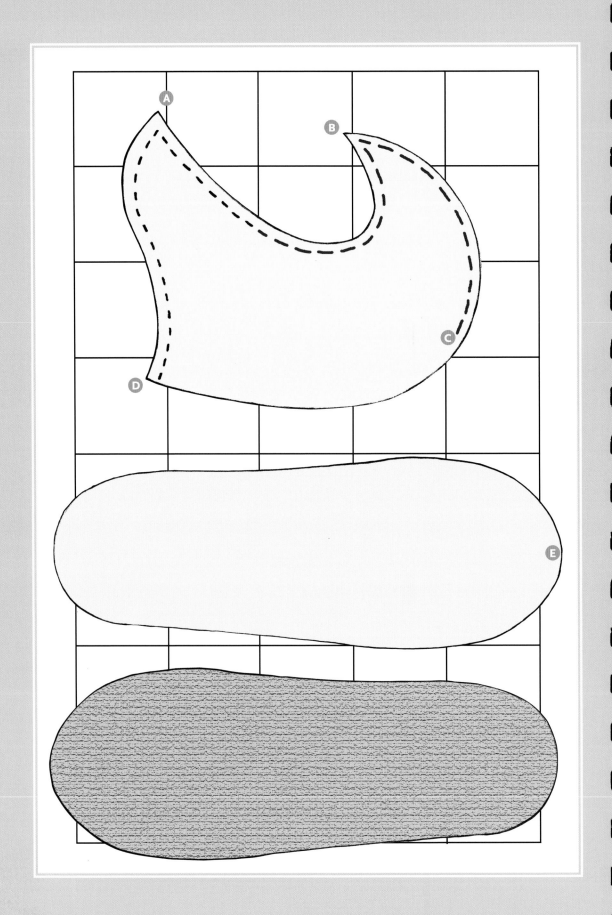

2 *On the right side of each of the side pieces, stitch from* **D** *to* **A** *. This stitching will give the slipper a more finished look and add more color.*

3 *Pin two of the side pieces together. Starting at* **A** *sew the side pieces together towards the toe and continue to* **C** *. Make a knot and trim. Sew about ¼" from the edge. Repeat for the second slipper. These are the tops of the slippers.*

4 *Spread open the two sewn side pieces. Match up* **C** *to* **E** *on the sole. Pin the side pieces to the soles. This may seem a little awkward at first, but you will soon see how quickly it makes a slipper! Again, stitch ¼" from the edge.*

5 *Sew the bells on the toes. The directions for sewing on a shank button (page 64) will show you how to sew on the bells. Or if you'd like, add small pom-poms or tassels. See pages 126–129.*

6 *When all the sewing is complete, glue on the non-slip soles. Follow the directions for the glue you have purchased. (They are not all the same.) Let the glue dry completely before you wear the slippers.*

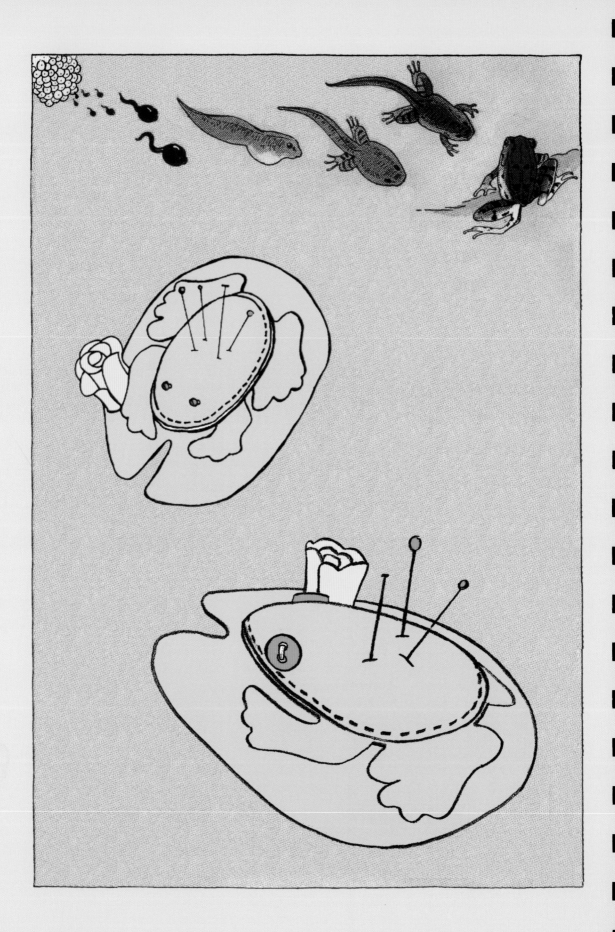

FROG PIN CUSHION

Frogs and lilies come in many different colors
so you can use whatever colors you like. I always
use two pin cushions—one for pins and one for needles.

MATERIALS: *3 pieces of felt (dark green 6 x 6", light
green at least 8 x 8", yellow 1 x 5"). Thread and
needle, stuffing, 2 beads or small buttons, and glue.*

DIRECTIONS: **1** *Copy pattern pieces on page 88 on a
copy machine and cut out. Pin the patterns onto the fabric.
Using a sharp but soft pencil, trace right along the edge of the pattern.
Remove the pins and cut out the shapes. Mark where the eyes are to
be sewn on the top of the body.*

The directions continue on the next page.

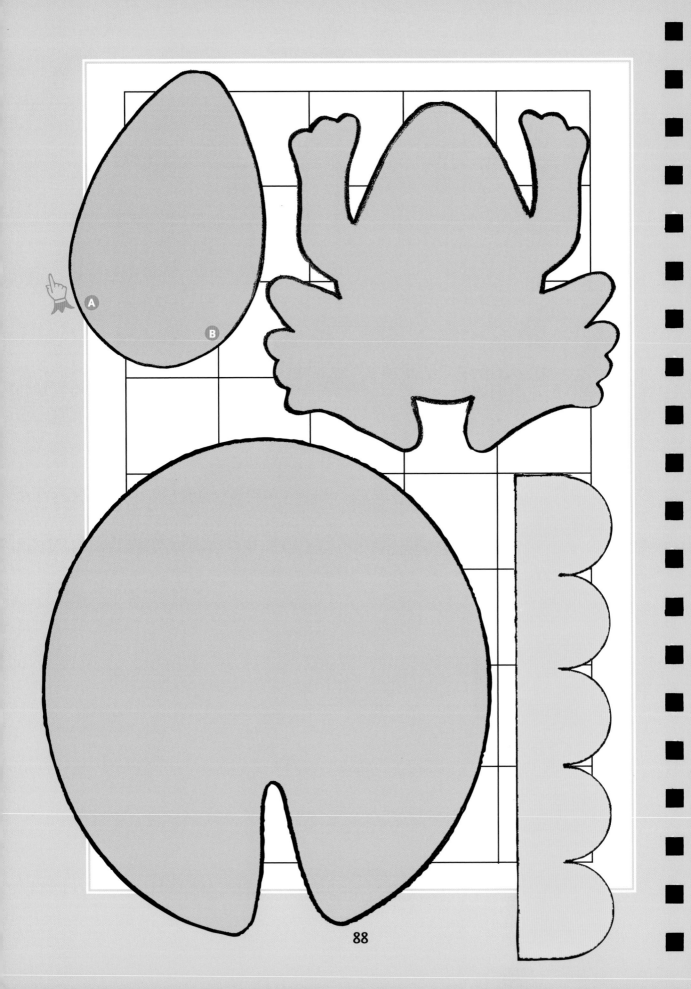

A B

2 *It will be easier to sew on the beads or embroider the eyes now, before you sew the body together. You could also embroider spots on the frog's back with French Knots (see page 52).*

3 *Pin the top of the frog (the plain oval) to the bottom of the frog. Baste them together (see page 42) so that the front and back edges match perfectly. Remove pins. Using green thread, sew from Ⓐ to Ⓑ. You want to leave an opening big enough to stuff the frog's body. Use your finger or the flat end of a pencil to push the stuffing into place. Do not use anything sharp as you don't want to tear the fabric or break the stitches. Remove basting thread.*

4 *Place the frog on the lily pad. Pin the back legs in position. Slide the front legs back slightly so that the frog's knees are up. Pin the front feet in place.*

5 *Remove back leg pins. Squeeze a drop of glue under each foot. Pin again to hold until dry. Glue the front feet in the same manner. Allow to dry completely before removing pins.*

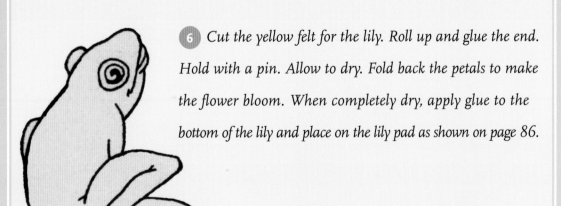

6 *Cut the yellow felt for the lily. Roll up and glue the end. Hold with a pin. Allow to dry. Fold back the petals to make the flower bloom. When completely dry, apply glue to the bottom of the lily and place on the lily pad as shown on page 86.*

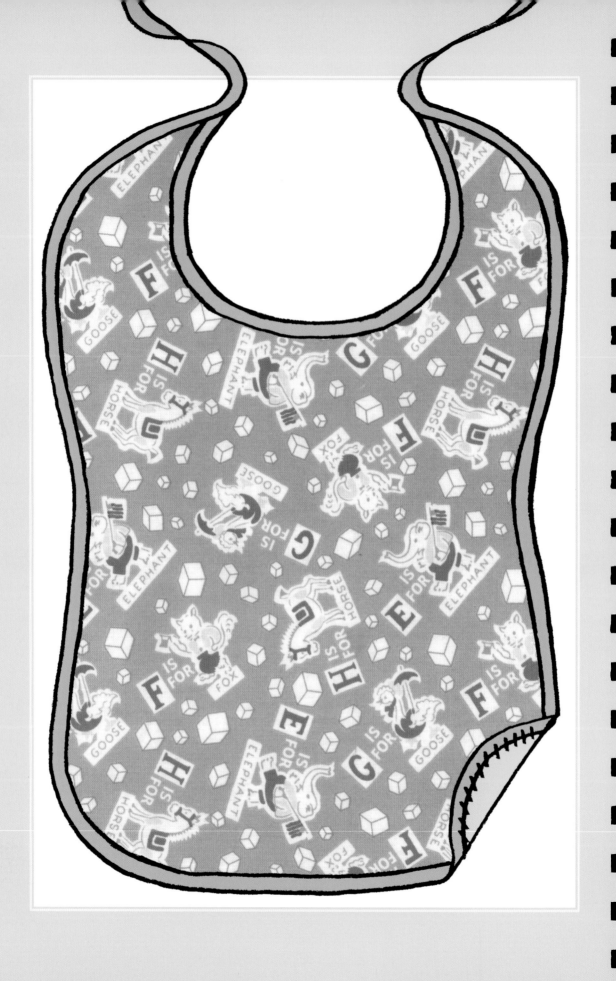

BABY'S BIB

A bib for a baby is an easy gift to make and a thoughtful gift. You can make it out of almost any fabric, even plastic! But keep in mind that it will be washed after every use.

MATERIALS: *A 12 x 16" piece of fabric, ½" seam binding, needle, thread, and whatever you decide to use to decorate (felt, embroidery thread, buttons).*

DIRECTIONS: **1** *Using a copy machine, enlarge the bib pattern on page 92 to 125 percent. Cut out the pattern.*

2 *Fold your material in half, lengthwise. Place the edge of the pattern marked* FOLD, *along the folded edge of the fabric. Pin the pattern along all the edges so the pattern cannot move.*

3 *Cut along the edge of the pattern, but do not cut the fabric along the lengthwise edge marked* FOLD. *When you are done cutting, remove the pins and lay the fabric flat.*

4 TO APPLY SEAM BINDING: *Fold the bib in half and mark the center of the neck at* **A** *with a soft pencil or tailor's chalk. Fold the seam binding for the neck in half and mark the center.*

5 *Lay the bib, right side facing you, on a flat surface. Unfold one side of the bias tape.*

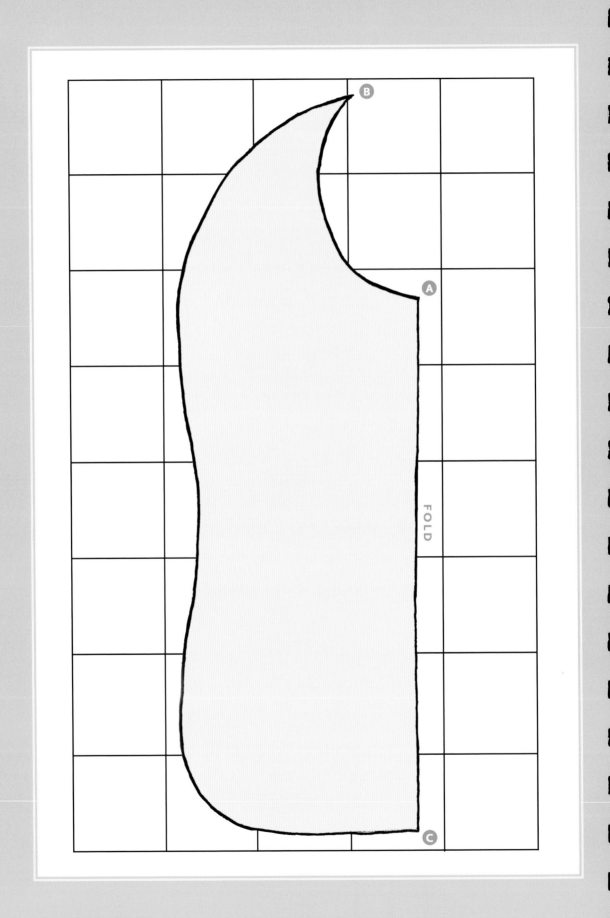

Match up the center of the tape and the center of the neck at (A). Starting at the center of the neck curve, pin the bias tape along the neck edge matching up the edge of the bib and the edge of the tape.

(6) Baste bias tape to the bib using the basting stitch (see page 42). Thread your needle. Knot the end and begin sewing at either corner of the bib at (B). Use the running stitch (see page 43) and sew in the crease of the tape. The stitches should be even and about ¼" in length. When you have sewn the tape to the entire neck curve, remove the basting.

(7) Now fold the still-folded edge of the bias tape over the top of the fabric towards the wrong side of the bib. The folded edge should just meet the back of the stitches you've just sewn. Since the tape is sewn, you don't have to pin the bias tape, but you should baste it to make sure it will stay flat as you stitch all around.

(8) Use the slip stitch (see page 47) to sew this folded edge to the back of the bib. Remove basting and trim the overhanging seam binding flush with the bib.

(9) Lay the bib flat in front of you, right side facing. Fold the binding tape in half and mark the center. Unfold one side of the bias tape. Match up the center of the tape and the center of the bib at the bottom at (C). Pin the bias tape to the bib matching up the edges all around. At each end you should have enough tape left over for the neck ties.

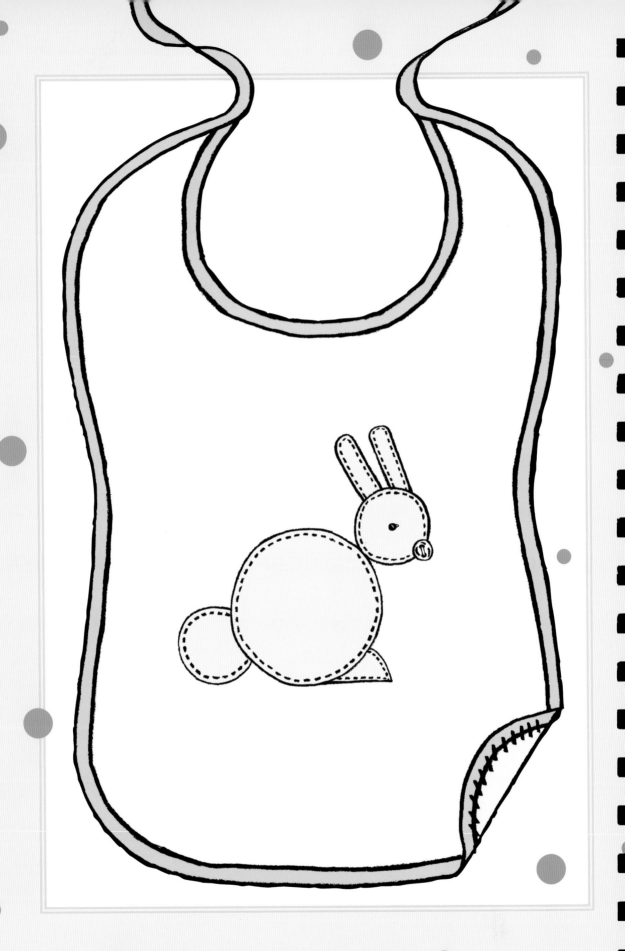

10 Beginning at **C** sew the seam binding to the outside edge of the bib in the same manner as you did for the neck, ending at **B** on each side. Don't worry about the neck ties, you will finish them later.

11 Now fold the still-folded edge of the bias tape over the top of the fabric to the wrong side of the bib. It should just meet the back of the stitches you've just sewn. Sew in the outside edge of the bib in the same manner as the neck from **C** to **B** .

12 Using the overhand stitch, sew the two edges of the binding tape together to close the neck ties.

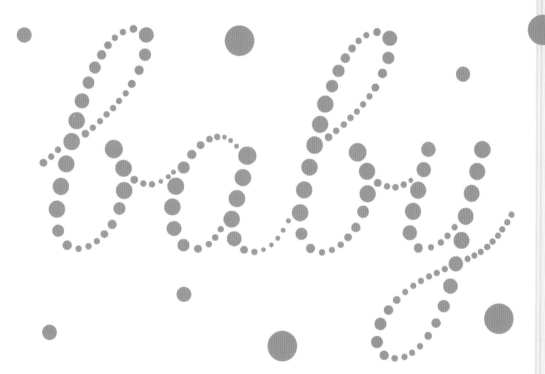

TO DECORATE THE BIB: *Of course, you can leave the bib perfectly plain, especially if you have used a lovely fabric. Or you can applique or embroider a design (see page 131), the baby's initials, or add the word "Baby."*

Then Mother made two feet.
She put them on the stocking.
She made two arms.
She put them on the stocking.
"It is a doll" cried Beverly.

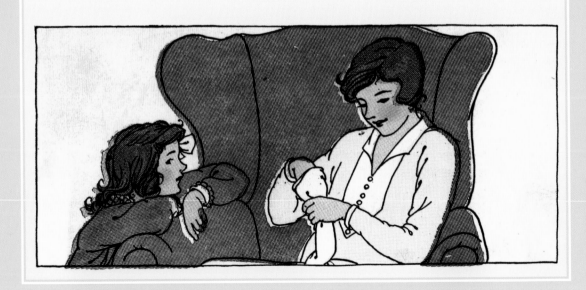

SOCK DOLL

The good news is . . . socks come in pairs! If you aren't completely happy with your first doll, you can make another one. Use an adult's sock for your first doll. The sock will make a bigger doll and provide more ribbing for the "legs." It will also be easier for little hands to work with. PLEASE NOTE: *The measurements given here are meant to serve as a guide. Not all socks are the same size. You will have to experiment and adjust these measurements for yourself.*

MATERIALS: *1 sock with a high cuff (not an anklet or short sock), cotton or fiberfill for stuffing, pins, scissors, needle, thread, string, felt, yarn, buttons, and a rubber band. If you are using a new sock, you might want to wash and dry it in advance to preshrink it.*

The directions begin on the next page.

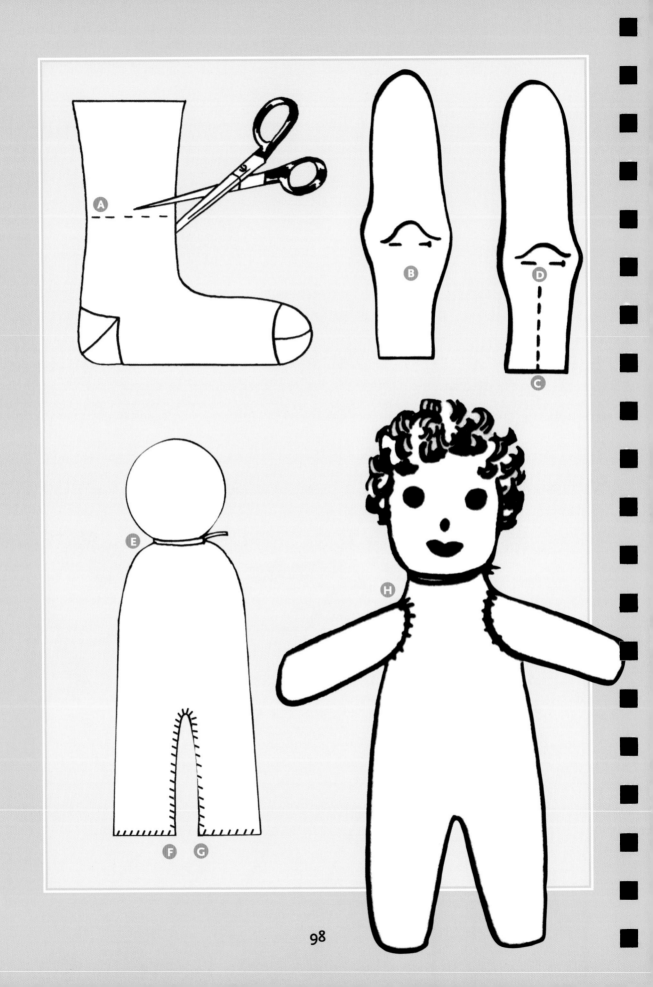

DIRECTIONS: *Pressing the sock with an iron will make it flat and easier to work with.*

(1) *Match up the top edges of the cuff. Mark the sock about 3" down from the cuff edge at* **(A)** *. Cut off this 3" section and set aside. This will form the arms.*

(2) *Lay the sock flat on a table with the heel facing you. Pin the heel up, away from the cuff edge as shown at* **(B)** *.*

(3) *Cutting from the cuff edge to the pin, cut the sock in two from* **(C)** *to* **(D)** *. This will form the two legs of the doll. Remove the pin from the heel.*

(4) *Measure 3" down from the toe. This is where you will wrap string to form the neck. Fill the head (the toe of the sock) with stuffing. Stuff it firmly so the head will have a good round shape, but don't overstuff. It will be difficult to handle if you are trying to keep the stuffing from popping out while working. When the stuffing has filled to the 3" mark, squeeze the sock together and wind the string around three or four times at* **(E)** *. Tie a knot and trim.*

(5) *Stuff the body below the neck in the same manner. When you get to the legs, pin the cut edges together. Using the hemming stitch (see page 46), start to sew at* **(F)** *then up and around to the bottom of the other leg at* **(G)** *. Make a knot and trim.*

(6) *Stuff the legs and sew up the bottoms (the feet). Again, make sure the stuffing is firm but not bursting out.*

7 *To make the arms, cut the cuff piece you set aside in half. Use the ribbing as a natural cutting line. Fold each piece in half, right sides together. Using the overhand stitch, sew one short end and then one long end. Make a knot and trim. Leave the other short end open. Turn the arm inside out. Stuff firmly. Sew and stuff the other arm in the same manner.*

8 *Sew the open end of the arm to the shoulders of the doll using the overhand stitch* **H** *.*

HAIR FOR YOUR SOCK DOLL: *These directions are for a simple braid and bangs.*

DIRECTIONS: **1** *Using a soft pencil, mark the top of the doll's forehead where the bangs will start and the braid will lay.*

2 **FOR THE BANGS**: *Cut ten pieces of yarn each 4" long. Fold each piece of yarn in half to create a loop. The loop end is where the yarn will be sewn to the doll's head.*

3 *Using all-purpose thread the same color as the hair, sew the looped end of the yarn pieces to the doll's forehead along the pencil line. The pieces of yarn will be too long, but you can trim them when you're all done.*

4 **FOR THE BRAID**: *Cut eighteen pieces of yarn each 16" long. Wind a rubber band around all the strands at one end to hold the strands together while you braid. Divide into thirds and braid all eighteen strands so that you have one long braid. Tie each end, trim evenly, and add a ribbon if you'd like.*

5 *Lay the braid over the top of the doll's head just covering the sewn loops of the bangs. Center the braid so that it is even on both sides. Sew the braid to the head.*

ADDING EYES AND MOUTH TO YOUR DOLL: *It is easier to place the eyes and mouth to the sock doll after you attach the hair. The hairline will show you exactly where the eyes should go. It is difficult to figure this out before the hair is attached. You can embroider the eyes or add buttons or beads instead. If the doll is for a small baby it is better to embroider the eyes and mouth so that buttons or beads cannot detach and be swallowed.*

CAP AND MITTENS

For this cap you make a pattern using your own head measuremer
use your own hand to determine the size of the mittens. Not only wi
these things yourself, but they will fit you perfectly! For this project, felt or polar fleece
will be the warmest and easiest fabrics to work with.

MITTEN MATERIALS: *A 12 x 16" piece of fabric, needle, craft thread or yarn, measuring tape or ruler, soft pencil or tailor's chalk, paper punch (if desired), ribbon (if desired).*

MITTEN DIRECTIONS: *Mittens of any size can be made from the pattern on page 104.* **1** *Lay your hand flat on the pattern and measure its length. Add ½" to the measurement to allow for seams all the way around the mitten. Compare the measurement to the pattern and then reduce or enlarge the pattern on a copy machine. If your hand plus the seam allowance is 20 percent larger than the pattern, for instance, enlarge the pattern to 120 percent.*

2 *Once you have determined the size of the mitten and copied it on the copy machine, cut it out. Pin to the fabric and, using a soft pencil or tailor's chalk, trace right along the line. You will need to cut out four. If you want to embroider or decorate the top of the mitten you should do it now, before sewing. Also, if you want to punch holes to put in a ribbon, you should do that now.*

3 *Using the blanket stitch (see page 53), start at either side of the wrist. Sew all the way around.*

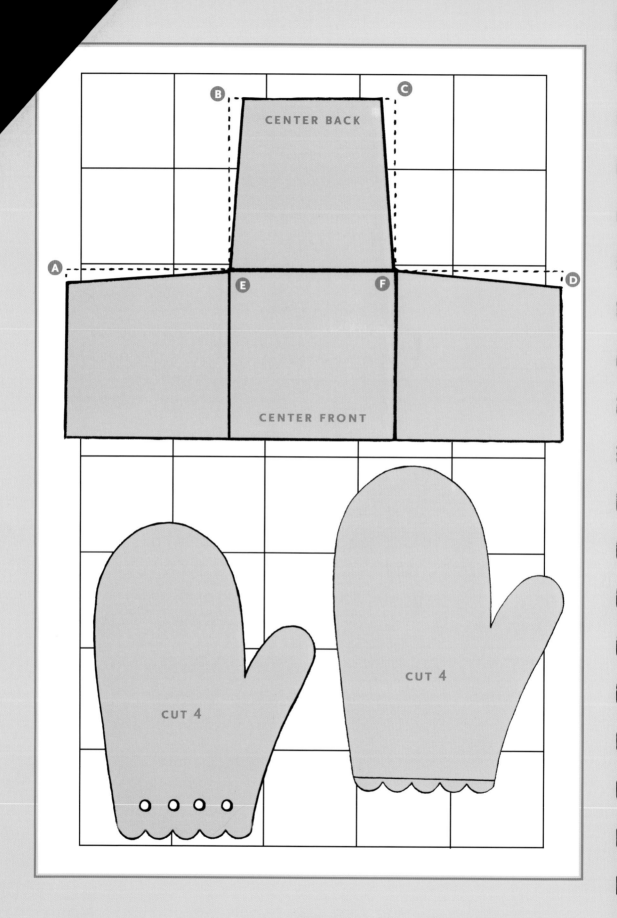

CENTER BACK

CENTER FRONT

CUT 4

CUT 4

CAP MATERIALS: *A 12 x 16" piece of fabric, ½" ribbon or seam binding, needle, craft thread or yarn, measuring tape, soft pencil or tailor's chalk.*

CAP DIRECTIONS: **1** *Measure your head by placing the measuring tape around your head just where a hat would sit. Cut a piece of paper the length of your headsize and half as wide. Fold the paper in half lengthwise then twice crosswise making a square. Now open the paper, you will have eight equal squares.*

2 *Cut off two squares on the short end. You will have six equal squares. This is your pattern. Cut out as shown on the drawing on page 104 tapering in ¼" at* **A** **B** **C** **D** *. Cut out the pattern and pin it to the fabric.*

3 *Using a soft pencil, trace right along the edge of the pattern onto the fabric. Remove the pins and cut out the cap. If you want to embroider a design or sew any decoration on to the cap, do it now before you sew the side seams. It will be much easier.*

4 *To sew the first side seam, bring* **A** *to* **B** *and line up the edges. Pin together then baste (see page 42). Remove pins. Starting at the neck edge and using the blanket stitch (see page 53), sew the seam towards the top of the cap* **E** *. When you get to the end, push the needle to the inside of the cap, make a knot, and trim so the knot doesn't show. Sew the other side seam in the same manner. Bring* **C** *to* **D** *and sew toward* **F** *.*

5 *Use the blanket stitch to sew all the unfinished edges. This is for decoration only. Cut the ribbon in half and sew one end of each ribbon to the inside of the cap.*

CAT PURSE

This is a pretty purse you can pin to whatever you are wearing. You can use it to hold your house or locker key as well as coins. Because all the edges are bound with a blanket stitch (see page 53) and will not fray, you can make it from almost any fabric. Once you understand how the cat is made, you can make your own design in any shape.

MATERIALS: *Felt (3 colors), 2 buttons for eyes, needle and thread, pencil, straight pins, safety pin, and scissors.*

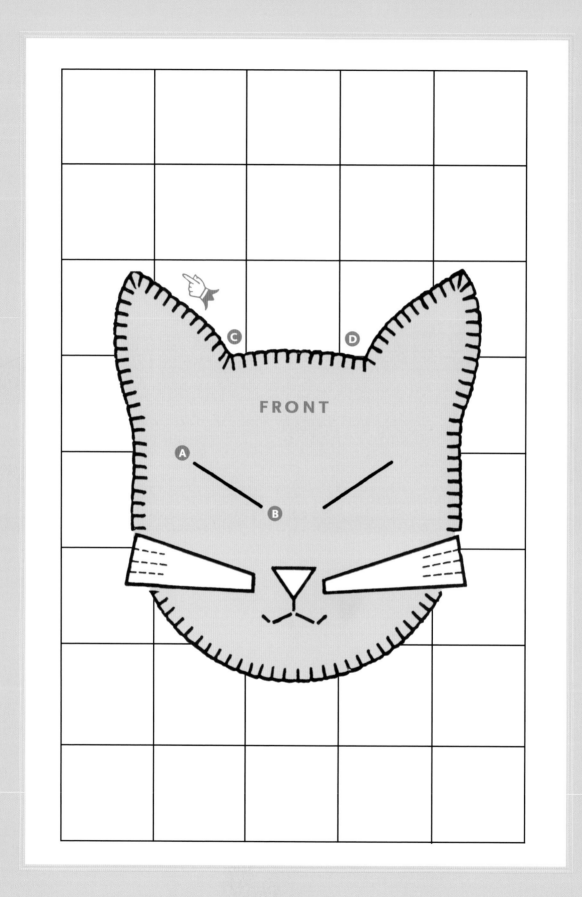

FRONT

DIRECTIONS: **1** *Copy the patterns on pages 108 and 110 on a copy machine. Cut out the patterns and pin to the fabric. Mark the position for the eyes and mouth by poking a soft pencil point through the paper pattern. Make an extra copy of the face pattern to use for the whiskers and nose. Pin the patterns to the fabric and trace all around. Remove the pins and cut out the pieces.*

2 *Cut the nose and whisker patterns out of the extra face pattern. Cut out two pieces for the whiskers. Slash the ends with a scissors to make a fringe. Use a different color felt for the nose. The mouth will be embroidered.*

3 *Now make the face. Cut slits from* **A** *to* **B** *for the buttonhole eyes and edge with the blanket stitch. Sew on the small triangular nose. Embroider the mouth and sew on the whiskers. Sew all around the outside of the face with a blanket stitch from* **C** *to* **D** *. The edge between the ears is not sewn.*

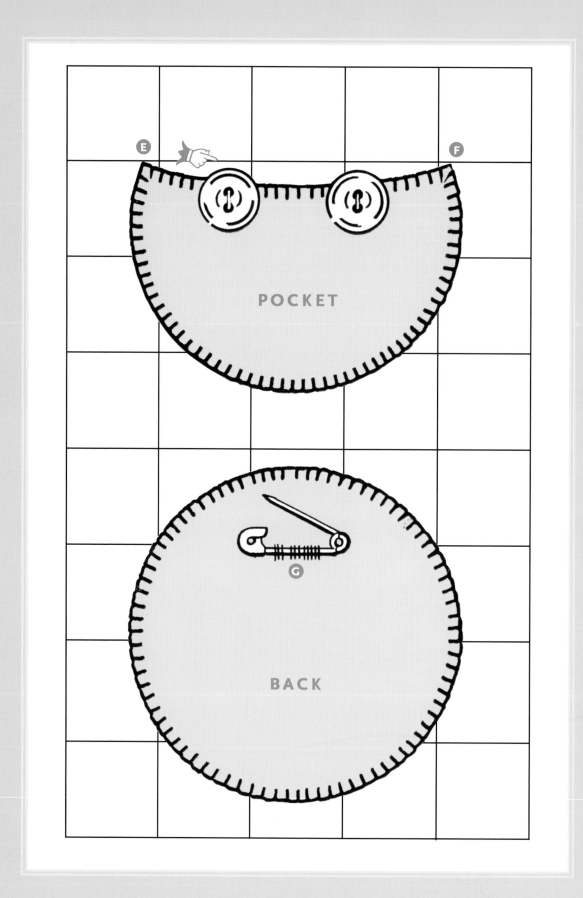

POCKET

BACK

E   F   G

④ *Make the pocket. First, sew blanket stitch across the top edge of the pocket from* ⑤ *to* ⑥ *. Then sew on two buttons for the eyes so that they correspond to the buttonholes on the face.*

⑤ *Attach the pocket to the back with the blanket stitch (see illustration below). Outline the entire edge of the back except the portion between the ears.*

⑥ *Sew the face to the pocket side of the back using the blanket stitch to the portion between the ears.*

⑦ *Sew a safety pin on the back above the center at* ⑥ *so that the purse will not tip when pinned on.*

EASY APRON

An apron is a useful thing to make. You can make it from almost any material, even plastic. Just bear in mind that an often-used apron is washed frequently. Think about how the apron will be used and how often it will be washed when choosing the material.

MATERIALS: *One 18" square of fabric (you can use a scarf or bandana), 1 package double-fold ½" bias tape or quilt binding, 36" of grossgrain ribbon or cloth tape, needle and thread.* NOTES: *If you plan to wash the apron (I can't imagine that you won't) you should preshrink the fabric by washing and drying it before sewing. Directions are given for edging the apron with bias tape. You could also hem all four sides. I prefer the bias tape because it adds color and gives a crisp look to the apron. You can also use the same color bias tape for the neck and waist ties.*

DIRECTIONS: **1** *Since the fabric is square, you can start at any corner. Unfold one side of the bias tape and match up the corner of the tape with the corner of the fabric. Pin the bias tape to the apron edge on all four sides. When you reach the corners, turn the bias tape at a 90 degree angle and start down the next side. See the illustration below. Leave ½" of bias tape overlapping at the end. You will need this to finish off the corner.*

2 *Baste bias tape to apron square using the basting stitch (see page 42). After all four sides have been basted, remove pins.*

3 *Thread your needle. Knot the end and begin sewing where you started. Using the running stitch (see page 43), sew right in the crease of the tape. The stitches should be even*

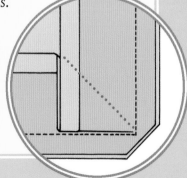

and about ¼" in length. Don't try to use one piece of thread for all four sides. It will be too long and will only get tangled. Use the usual arm's length of thread. You may have to rethread two or three times.

④ *When you're about 1½" away from the end, stop sewing and fold in ½" overhang. Tuck it under to line it up with the beginning edge. Fold over the other side and pin to secure. Pick up your needle and continue sewing to the end. Knot and trim. Remove the basting.*

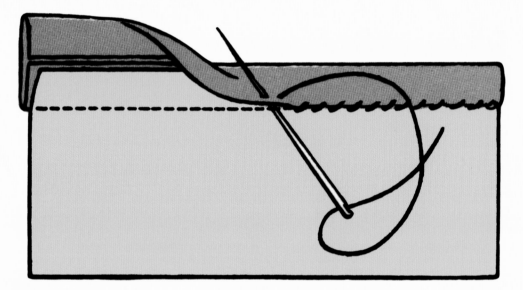

⑤ *Now fold the still-folded edge of the bias tape over the top of the fabric to the wrong side of the fabric. It should just meet the back of the stitches you've just sewn. Since one side of the tape is sewn, you don't have to pin the bias tape, but you should baste it to make sure it will stay flat as you stitch around all four sides.*

⑥ *Using the slip stitch (see page 47), sew this folded edge to the back of the apron. See illustration above. See the illustration on page 113 for how to turn the corners. After you have sewn the other side of the bias tape, press the apron square on all four sides.*

7 *Lay the apron square flat on a surface in front of you, right side facing. Put the corner where you started and finished at the bottom, closest to you.*

8 *From the point of the top corner, measure down 6" on each side. Mark with a pin. Fold the corner down creating a triangular bib on the front of the apron. Pin and press.*

9 *Cut two pieces of ribbon or tape, 12" each. Fold the end ¼" and sew to the back side of the bib, just where it is folded down.*

10 *Cut another two pieces of ribbon or tape for the waist ties. To determine exactly where the waist ties should go, put the apron on and tie the neck ties. Mark with a soft pencil where the waist ties will sit comfortably. Fold the end ¼" and sew to the sides of the apron.*

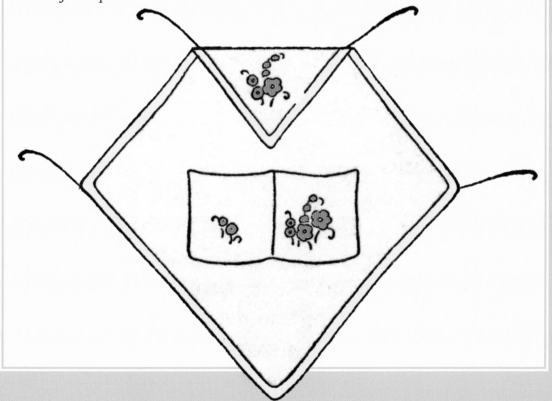

SEWING CARDS

tulip

SEWING CARDS
AND
DESIGNS FOR EMBROIDERY

Sewing cards are a great way to practice the basic sewing and embroidery stitches. You can use some of the designs here or you can make your own cards using your own designs. Use a copy machine to copy these or your own designs on to card stock. (Normal copy paper is too light and flimsy to sew.) Or, you can copy the designs on a copy machine, cut them out along the edge of the picture, and trace right along the edge on to fabric. These pictures are wonderful, but the ones you draw yourself are even better.

bird

squirrel

pansy

bunny

swan

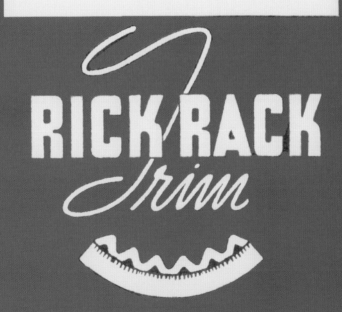

FINISHES
AND
TRIMS

RICK RACK
Trim

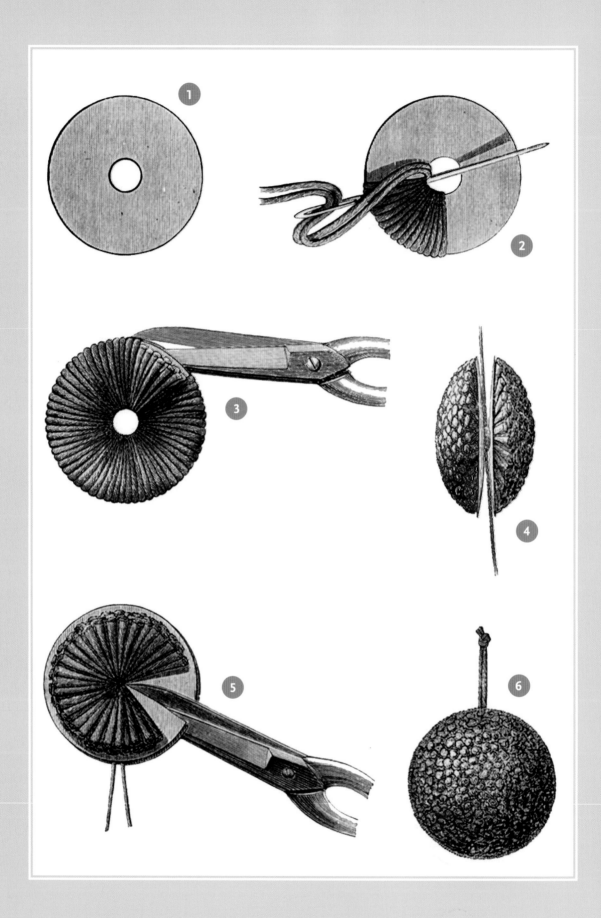

HOW TO MAKE A POM-POM

Pom-poms are easy to make. You can sew or tie them to many of the projects in this book (like the Elf Slippers on page 83) or attach them to items you already have. You will need to use a material with thickness and spring, so that the pom-poms puff out properly.

MATERIALS: *A sheet of cardboard, yarn.*

DIRECTIONS: **1** *Cut two cardboard circles, about 2¼" in diameter. Cut a hole in the center of each circle, about ½" wide.*

2 *While holding the circles together, wind yarn around the two circles until they are firmly and fully wound with yarn. A large yarn needle will make it easier to guide the yarn through the center hole.*

3 *Slip the point of the scissors between the two cardboard circles and clip the yarn carefully all the way around the edges. Don't worry about the unfinished pom-pom falling apart, the cardboard will hold the cut yarn until you tie it.*

4 *Place a length of yarn between the two cardboard circles and wind around the yarn going through the center hole. Tie tightly around the yarn and make a knot.*

5 *Cut through the circles to make removing them easier. Slide both circles off the yarn.*

6 *The finished pom-pom is ready to sew or tie.*

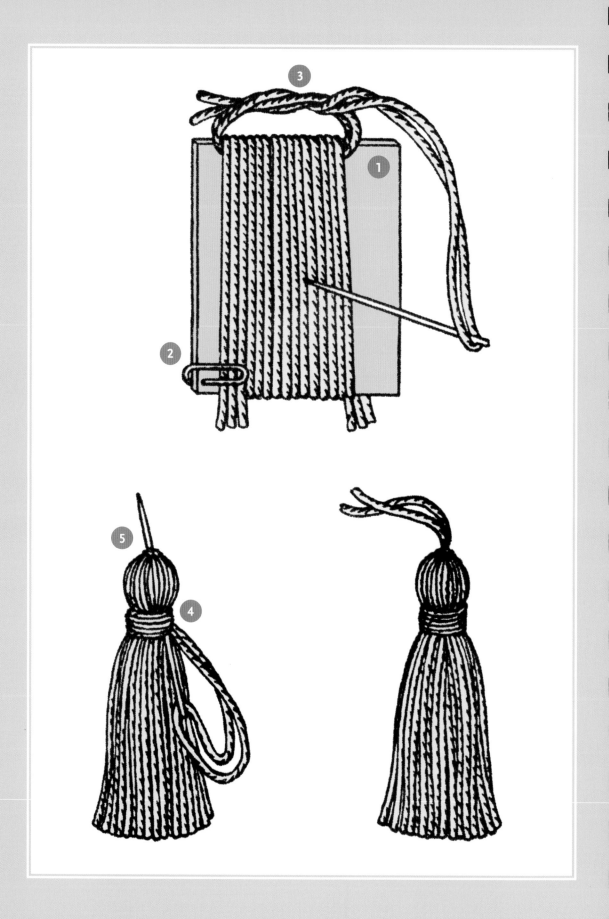

HOW TO MAKE A TASSEL

Tassels are even easier to make than pom-poms. You can sew or tie them to many of the projects in this book (like the Elf Slippers on page 83) or attach them to items you already have. Like pom-poms, you can make them out of many different materials. Unlike pom-poms, you can use a wider variety of materials for tassels. They don't have to be thick or springy. Yarn will make a fluffy tassel, thread a much thinner one.

MATERIALS: *A sheet of cardboard, yarn.*

DIRECTIONS: **1** *Cut a piece of cardboard that is as long as you want your tassel to be. Make it about 2" wide.*

2 *Wind the strands of thread or yarn evenly around the cardboard until you have the bulk you want. You can hold the end with a paper clip.*

3 *Thread a needle with a piece of the yarn and draw it under the yarn. Bring the ends together and tie a knot.*

4 *Cut the yarn at the bottom of the cardboard. Take the yarn you used to tie the top knot and wind it four or five times around the yarn, about ½" below the top, to bind the tassel together.*

5 *Thread a needle with the two ends and slip it inside the top of the tassel as shown. Use the two threads to tie or sew the tassel to your project.*

MONOGRAMS

A monogram is a decoration using the initials of a name or the name itself. Adding a monogram is a wonderful way to decorate items you've either made yourself—or not. You can put your monogram on towels, baby bibs, hankies, scarves, bed linens, etc. You can even embroider the date to mark a special occasion. Monogramming is usually done with embroidery stitches and embroidery thread, but you can also use bias tape or ribbon as shown on the opposite page.

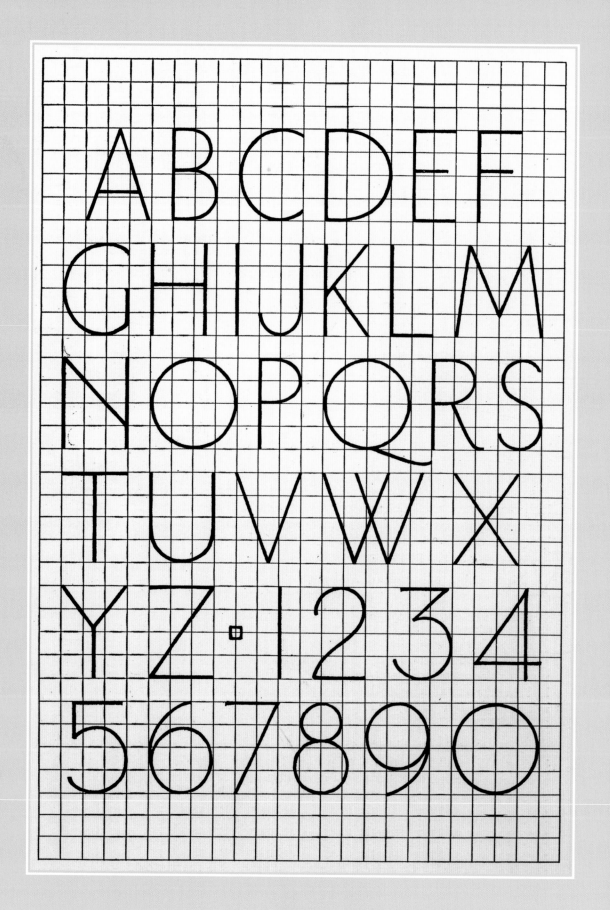

A B C D E

F G H I J K

L M N

O P Q R S T U

V W X Y Z &c

abcdefghyklmnopqrsstuvwxyzz

A B C D

E F G H

I J K L

MNOR

STUV

WXYZ

A Q A B B C D E
F G G H I J K L M
N O P Q R S T Z
U V V W W X Y Z
& $ 1 2 3 4 5 6 7
8 9 0 a b c d e f g
h i j k l m n o p q
r ſ s t u v w x y z
. , - ` ' : ; ! ?

A B C D

E F G H I

J K L M

N O P Q R

S T U V

W X Y Z

A B C D

J K L M

S T U V

E F G H I

N O P Q R

W X Y Z

Notes for my Sewing

Notes for my Sewing

Notes for my Sewing

Notes for my Sewing

Notes for my Sewing

Notes for my Sewing

PICTURE CREDITS

Page 49 Encyclopedia of Needlework ©1963 Hearthside Press, Inc., New York. **Page 50** See and Sew by Mariska Karasz Illustrations by Christine Engler ©1943 J. B. Lippincott Company Philadelphia, New York. **Page 51** The Sew-It Book by Rachel Taft Dixon, Illustrated by Marjorie Hartwell and Rachel Taft Dixon ©1929 Rand McNally & Company, New York, Chicago, San Francisco. **Page 53** Sew Simple. **Page 55** The Girl's Book of Sewing by Jane Chapman, Illustrations by Walter Chapman and Jeva Cralick ©1952 Greenburg:Publisher, New York. **Page 57** (top) The Sew-It Book by Rachel Taft Dixon, Illustrated by Marjorie Hartwell and Rachel Taft Dixon ©1929 Rand McNally & Company, New York, Chicago, San Francisco, (bottom) Needlecraft Magazine ©Needlecraft Publishing Company, Augusta, Maine. **Page 58** (top)Sew Simple, (bottom) Let's Learn to Sew by James Norbury ©1953 The Bodley Head London. **Page 62** Childcraft ©1954 Field Enterprises, Inc. **Page 63** (top) The Home Educator ©1923 W. F. Quarrie & Company, Chicago, (bottom) Encyclopedia of Needlework ©1963 Hearthside Press, Inc., New York. **Page 64** Let's Learn to Sew by James Norbury ©1953 The Bodley Head London. **Page 66** Needlecraft Magazine, May ©1928 Needlecraft Publishing Company, Augusta, Maine. **Page 68** The Sewing Book ©1913 The Butterick Publishing Conmpany, New York. **Page 69** The Sew-It Book by Rachel Taft Dixon, Illustrated by Marjorie Hartwell and Rachel Taft Dixon ©1929 Rand McNally & Company, New York, Chicago, San Francisco. **Page 70** Illustrations by Ellie Brickman. **Pages 72–73** Illustrations from HOW TO SEW by Nina R. Jordan, Illustrated by the Author ©1941 and renewed 1969 by Nina R. Jordan, reproduced by permission of Harcourt, Inc. **Page 74** Illustration by Ellie Brickman. **Page 78** Dishes with Dash: 57 Ways of Using Heinz Tomato Ketchup and Heinz Tomato Chutney by A. H. Adair ©H. J. Heinz Company Ltd., London. **Page 79** (top) Illustration by Ellie Brickman, (bottom) Household Arts for Home and School by Anna M. Cooley and Wilhelmina H. Spohr ©1929 The Macmillan Company, New York. **Pages 80–82** Illustrations by Ellie Brickman. **Page 83** Friends: A Primer ©1929 Mary E. Pennell and Alice M. Cusack. **Page 84** Illustrations by Ellie Brickman. **Page 86** (top)Elson-Gray Basic Readers, Book 3 by William H. Elson and William S. Gray ©1931 Scott, Foresman and Company, Chicago, New York, (bottom) Illustrations by Ellie Brickman. **Page 87** Illustrations by Ellie Brickman. **Page 88** Number Fun by Edna M. Aldredge and Jessie F. McKee, Illustrated by Eileen Fox ©1932 The Harter Publishing Company, Cleveland, Ohio. **Page 90** Fabric: 30's Playtime by Moda. **Pages 90, 92, 94** Illustrations by Ellie Brickman. **Page 96** Friends: A Primer ©1929 Mary E. Pennell and Alice M. Cusack. **Pages 97–101** Illustrations by Ellie Brickman. **Page 102** (left) The Complete Book of Sewing by Constance Talbot ©1943 Book Presentation, New York, (right) Illustrations by Ellie Brickman. **Page 104** Illustrations by Ellie Brickman. **Pages 106–111** Childcraft ©1954 Field Enterprises, Inc. **Page 112** (upper right and upper left)Illustrations from HOW TO SEW by Nina R. Jordan, Illustrated by the Author ©1941 and renewed 1969 by Nina R. Jordan, reproduced by permission of Harcourt, Inc., (lower left) How to Make Children's Clothes the Modern Singer Way. The Singer Sewing Machine Co., Inc. **Page 114** Simplicity Sewing Book ©1953 Simpliciity Pattern Co., Inc. New York. **Page 115** The Big Book of Needlecraft ©1937 Odhams Press, Ltd., London. **Page 116** Home Arts Needlecraft Magazine ©1936 Needlecraft Publishing Company, Augusta, Maine. **Page 117** (top) Pictures to Sew, Illustrations D & D Downs ©1942 The Saalfield Publishing Company, Akron, Ohio, (bottom) Stories about Lina and Lee by Eleanor Thomas ©1949 Ginn and Company, Phillipines. **Pages 118–123** Coping Saw Carpentry by Edwin T. Hamilton, Illustrations by G. Ruth Taylor ©1934 The Harter Publishing Company, Cleveland, Ohio. **Page 124** Good Housekeeping's Complete Book of Needlecraft by Vera P. Guild ©1959 The Hearst Corporation, New York. **Page 126** Encyclopedia of Needlework by Therese de Dillmont. **Page 128** Sewing Simplified by Mary Brooks Picken ©1938. 1939, 1940 by Mary Brooks Picken. **Page 130** Wright's Bias Fold Tape ©1932 Wm. E. Wright & Sons Co., New Jersey. **Page 131** Modern Home Sewing by Drucella Lowrie and Sylvia Mager ©1952 Home Arts Associates and Sylvia K. Mager. **Pages 134–135** Needlecraft Encyclopedia ©1947 Stamford House, New York. **Page 136** The Book of American Types ©1941 American Typefounders Sales Corporation, New Jersey. **Page 137** Modern Alphabets by Melbert B. Cary, Jr. ©1930 Bridgman Publishers, New York. **Pages 140–145** The Type Book ©Advertising Agencies Service Company, New York. **Page 148** Child Life, July 1931 © Rand McNally & Company, New York, Chicago, San Francisco. **Page 149** The Sew-It Book by Rachel Taft Dixon, Illustrated by Marjorie Hartwell and Rachel Taft Dixon ©1929 Rand McNally & Company, New York, Chicago, San Francisco. **Endpaper** (back)Mill Engraving ©The Design Library, Wappinger's Falls, New York. **Cover** (back) Needlecraft Magazine, May ©1928 Needlecraft Publishing Company, Augusta, Maine.

ACKNOWLEDGMENTS

I would like to thank the following people for their help and encouragement: Ellie Brickman, Gina Federico, Bea Feitler, Ruth Anne Flore, Sallie Gouverneur, Erica Halivni, Linda Hill, Mariah Hughs, Dor, Haggit, and Oz Lin, Andrea Meislin, Betsey Miller, Amy Newman, Barbara Richer, Nancy Rosen, Mary Savino, Virginia Siedel, Ruth Sorensen, Daniel, Lily, and James Snyder(more than I hoped for, better than I deserve), Dervla Kelly, Leslie Stoker, Bradbury Thompson, and Linda Zisquit. As always, special thanks to my mother, Bernice Sapirstein Davis, who sewed all my baby clothes.

CLARENCE BIERS

All done, thank you.

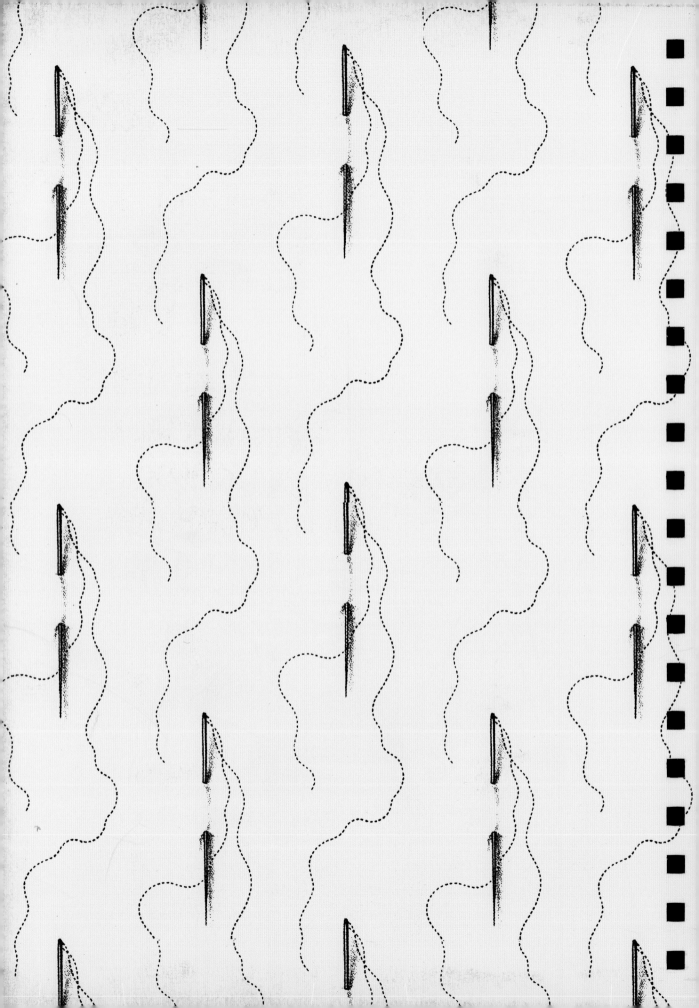